T0305105

Transnational Corporations in Southeast Asia

NEW HORIZONS IN INTERNATIONAL BUSINESS

General Editor: Peter J. Buckley
Professor of Managerial Economics
Management Centre, University of Bradford

This series is aimed at the frontiers of international business research. Each volume tackles key problem areas in international political economy. The study of international business is important not least because it gives researchers the opportunity to innovate in theory, technique, empirical investigation and interpretation. The area is fruitful for interdisciplinary and comparative research. This series is established as a central forum for the presentation of new ideas in international business.

New Directions in International Business
Research Priorities for the 1990s
Edited by Peter J. Buckley

Europe and the Multinationals
Issues and Responses for the 1990s
Edited by Stephen Young and James Hamill

Multinational Enterprises in the World Economy
Essays in Honour of John Dunning
Edited by Peter J. Buckley and Mark Casson

Multinational Investment in Modern Europe
Strategic Interaction in the Integrated Community
Edited by John Cantwell

The Growth and Evolution of Multinational Enterprise
Patterns of Geographical and Industrial Diversification
R.D. Pearce

Multinational Enterprise and Public Policy
A Study of the Industrial Countries
A.E. Safarian

Transnational Corporations in Southeast Asia
An Institutional Approach to Industrial Organization
Hans Jansson

European Integration and Competitiveness
Acquisitions and Alliances in Industry
Edited by Frédérique Sachwald

Transnational Corporations in Southeast Asia

An Institutional Approach to Industrial Organization

Hans Jansson
Professor
Institute of Economic Research
School of Economics and Management
Lund University

Edward Elgar

Published by
Edward Elgar Publishing Limited
Gower House
Croft Road
Aldershot
Hants GU11 3HR
England

Edward Elgar Publishing Company
Old Post Road
Brookfield
Vermont 05036
USA

British Library Cataloguing in Publication Data

Jansson, Hans
Transnational Corporations in Southeast Asia: An Institutional Approach to Industrial Organization. – (New Horizons in International Business Series)
I. Title II. Series
338.80959

Library of Congress Cataloguing-in-Publication Data

Jansson, Hans
Transnational corporations in Southeast Asia: an institutional approach to industrial organization/Hans Jansson
p. cm. – (New horizons in international business)
Includes bibliographical references and index.
1. International business enterprises–Asia, Southeastern–Case studies. 2. Corporations, European–Asia, Southeastern–Case studies. 3. Industrial organization–Asia, Southeastern–Case studies.
I. Title. II. Series.
HD2901.J36 1994
338.8'8859–dc20 93–32247
CIP

ISBN 1 85278 983 2
Printed on FSC approved paper
Printed and bound in Great Britain by Marston Book Services Ltd, Oxfordshire

Contents

List of Figures

List of Tables

Preface

During many years spent in studying the operations of Western European transnational corporations (TNCs) in Southern and Eastern Asia I have become increasingly aware of the large differences there are between the ways of doing business in Asia and in Western Europe. The differences remain great despite a continual increase in the internationalization of the world's economy and the fact that Europeans and Asians are coming closer to each other all the time. These Asian countries also differ among themselves in their business cultures. Common to all is a rather low level of industrialization. European TNCs, as well, differ in their approach to doing business in the area. Some made heavy investments there, whereas others have simply followed the crowd, their business there being of marginal importance to them. Although the TNCs active in the region have adapted to local conditions, this has not seemed to have meant their losing their European identity and 'going Asian'. The adaptation of such corporations does not usually go so far that their basic framework is markedly changed.

Mainstream theories on the operations of TNCs have tended to be conceived in a somewhat superficial way, the differences between various TNCs in their operations being explained, not by taking precise account of local circumstances and the culture of the firm, but by dealing in a more general way with the industrial environment, the market of the country, matters of technology, and the like. It seems to be expected that some general theory concerned with the behavioural characteristics of all TNCs will be adequate here. Such a theory, to be sure, may suffice for examining Western TNCs in the market environments of the industrialized market economies in which they originated. However, for illuminating the operations of such firms in an Asian environment basically foreign to them and comparing their operations there with those of Asian TNCs, a different type of theory is needed. The dominant business system in Southeast Asia is strongly influenced by the Chinese, Japanese and Korean companies located there. Although these companies have emulated Western business practices in many ways, this has not affected the 'inner core' of these firms appreciably. Thus, there are very basic differences between

European TNCs, even as regards their Southeast Asian subsidiaries, and companies stemming from Eastern Asia directly. In this book an institutional approach will be used to provide insight into the differences alluded to between various firms and markets. This will involve examining the institutional background of Western European TNCs within the very special Southeast Asian context. This aims at providing a deeper understanding of the institutional origin of these companies.

The puzzle of regional and local differences in the approaches taken to business matters has led to my focusing on various theoretical problems that are thus implicated and to my endeavouring to bring together and integrate various theories of TNCs with the hope of developing some unified theory of the TNC as an economic institution. Gaining as thorough insight as possible into the operations of such firms in Southeastern Asia seemed to me of utmost importance in this connection. Whatever the reader's concern it is hoped that this latter aspect will also make the book interesting to a reader primarily concerned with knowing more about the problems in Southeast Asia and about how Western European TNCs can best prepare themselves for doing business in the region.

In a comprehensive empirical investigation of long duration, fruitful and long-term contacts with those TNCs of interest were essential. I am heavily indebted indeed to my interviewees at the subsidiaries of these TNCs in Southeast Asia who have shared their experience with me during my many visits there.

I also want to thank my colleagues at the School of Economics and Management of Lund University who have assisted in the preparation of the book, particularly Sven-Olof Collin, Ulf Elg, Ulf Johansson and Rikard Larsson, whose comments and criticisms have stimulated the reworking of substantial portions of the text. I am heavily indebted to Robert W. Goldsmith, who not only assisted me in correcting my English but also helped me to remove different errors and obscurities in the argumentation.

A grant from the Swedish Council for Research in the Humanities and Social Sciences assisted me in the initial stages of research, while the financial assistance given by the South Swedish Chamber of Commerce (*Stiftelsen för främjande av ekonomisk forskning vid Lunds universitet*) made it possible for me to finalize the book. I wish to express my deep appreciation to Maj-Britt Johansson, who did a valiant and professional job in her typing and editing of the book and Lena Hansson for her professional job of typing certain parts of it.

1. Transnational Corporations in Southeast Asia

The group management of a large transnational corporation (TNC) based in Europe decided to sell out one of its many product lines. No major problems were foreseen in implementing this decision. Indeed, since the firm's global organization was divisionalized according to product type and most of its worldwide subsidiaries belonged to one of these product divisions, the relative independence of which could be seen as representing one of the major advantages of a divisionalized organization of this sort, it was thought to be easy enough for the firm to break out this product-line from the others. However, implementation of this top-level decision was not as easy as had been expected. Protests soon surfaced from unexpected parts of the global organization, namely from several of the Asian subsidiaries. For one of these companies, such a divestment would have meant not only losing more than half its business, and with this a major contribution to its common overhead, but also the local business culture, based on the company's offering an integrated mix of different products, being disrupted. For such multi-product companies, there may be a critical mass concerning the variety that a product portfolio must involve for the company to succeed. Subsidiaries of this sort tend to be linked to product-line companies in a different way than are single-product subsidiaries located in larger and less remote markets. In the case in hand, a compromise was finally reached, the product-line in Europe being sold but that in Asia being kept.

A Southeast Asian sales subsidiary of another large TNC found itself to be in bad shape. Careful examination of its business revealed negligence in local marketing and service, high employee turnover, frequent changes in the managing directors, and losses for the previous five years. The gravity of the situation was first realized when a large distributor in a nearby country was transferred from this sales subsidiary to another, located in Northeast Asia. It became evident that nearly all the profits the sales subsidiary had reported for the past several years had come from this distributor and not from the local market. This had made the subsidiary complacent, since it had not needed to earn its own profits. A major reason for these serious problems being hidden for so long was that the group had lost much of its control over the subsidiary several years earlier when it had dismantled the regional organization.

This second case illustrates the difficulties a complex worldwide organization can have in controlling its small sales subsidiaries located in remote markets. The group's business operations in Southeast Asia had for the most part been established during the first half of the 1980s through the building up of a market organization consisting of distributors and sales subsidiaries. Business had been managed from a centrally located subsidiary, which had served as a regional office. After the establishment period was completed, this regional function was taken away. This coincided with a change in managing directors and the start of a deep recession in the area. After a period of build-up and support from the group, the subsidiaries had been left to manage on their own.

Both these cases illustrate the fact that subsidiaries in small and distant markets are often organized and controlled differently than are subsidiaries in major European markets. The cases also illustrate the problems which can result from insufficient knowledge at the central level regarding local developments in Eastern Asian subsidiaries. With the rapid growth of business in the area, such problems are becoming increasingly serious and are influencing more and more the global organization of TNCs. In an earlier study (Jansson, 1993), the author found problems of this sort to be typical of those experienced by European TNCs in the extension of their operations into Eastern Asia in efforts to take advantage of the tremendous business opportunities created by the rapid economic developments there. That part of the world is largely unknown territory with exciting strategic and organizational challenges not faced within the traditional markets of Europe and North America. This surge of Asian investment represents a third wave of global penetration, in the sense of the first wave of internationalization having taken the companies out of their home countries into other parts of Western Europe and the second wave involving investment in North America. Their expansion into Eastern Asia made the TNCs global in a more real sense, now operating in all of these major world markets, with one leg at each corner of a triad, so to speak. Due to the present and future importance of these markets, the extension of these TNCs into Eastern Asia represents a major strategic move on their parts. The prophecy of the Pacific Ocean being the economic hub of the future seems well founded. The region will surely increasingly become the home market and the 'backyard' of competitors from both the big dragon Japan herself and from the smaller dragons of South Korea, Taiwan, Hong Kong and Singapore, as well as the 'minidragons' of Thailand, Malaysia and Indonesia.

This third wave of investment poses major strategic and organizational problems for many European TNCs. Important to them is not simply to establish and maintain profitable business operations in the area, based on their existing assets and their competitive advantages gained elsewhere, but also to integrate these new business operations into their global strategies and global organization. The challenge this represents is the focus of the book. This challenge requires that a trade-off be made between local business goals and goals of global integration. How well a TNC meets this challenge is a test of its ability to create a truly functioning 'transnational organization' as described by Bartlett and Ghoshal (1989) or 'multi-dimensional organization' as it is called in this book.

Eastern Asian markets have a strongly local character, one which must be adequately understood in order that operations there can be adequately coordinated with the operations in the TNC as a whole, allowing economies of scale and scope to be taken advantage of. This has introduced new dimensions into the present and future operations of European TNCs, and has had the two following effects.

First, it has made the question of a group's responsiveness to local conditions an important issue. No longer can investments in such regions outside the major markets be seen as being of marginal importance. Rather, the problem of integrating local business units with two major components of the global organization of a TNC, namely its global product divisions and its group management, are viewed as having a significant impact on the group as a whole.

Second, it has highlighted the importance of TNCs expanding into new geographical areas and broadening their perspectives regarding such functions as marketing, production, and purchasing, or such organizational issues as that of the integration of corporate cultures.

Although the prime emphasis is placed here on the organizational problems inherent in this expansion into the local markets of the Southeast Asian region, consideration of these organizational problems is not complete without going into other issues, such as those of the marketing, manufacturing and purchasing strategies these TNCs pursue in this geographical area, and of how the TNCs have established themselves there.

THE LOCAL PERSPECTIVE

To become acquainted with the problems that the TNCs face in their expansion into Southeast Asia, the local operations of 17 European TNCs were studied in relation to the overall strategy, goals and organizational make-up of the TNCs. The subsidiaries of the TNCs considered were ones in the major ASEAN countries (Singapore, Malaysia, Thailand, Indonesia, and the Philippines), or in Southeast Asia (SEA) as this group of countries will, somewhat improperly, be referred to here.

The subsidiaries in question are ones located far from the group headquarters in Europe. Their remoteness in relation to their groups can be considered both in terms of physical (geographic) distance and in terms of psychic distance, mainly due to dissimilarity in operating conditions. The distance from headquarters, and from industrially mature countries, which is partly physical and partly psychic, involves at least five different aspects:

1. The markets and the market institutions are different.
2. The cultural and social values are different.
3. The level of technology utilized by customers and by suppliers is lower.
4. The infrastructure is often deficient, as seen by European standards.
5. Governments are much more involved in the control of business operations than is usually the case in Europe or the US.

For these and other reasons, the organizational problems in these markets tend to be extreme. Distance creates uncertainty in many ways. The problems that result pose a number of questions. How should TNCs organize the local business operations of such far-off subsidiaries in less industrialized countries (LICs)? How will the organization of the overall group be influenced? How can the interests of national responsiveness/differentiation and those of global coordination/integration be reconciled?

Transactions in markets that are highly remote appear to be controlled differently from transactions in markets nearby. Thus, transactions in remote markets are presumably harder for the TNC organization to coordinate and to integrate with transactions of the group as a whole. It can be assumed to be especially difficult to involve subsidiaries located in remote markets in the long-range global integration of research and development activities with those of production and marketing. Possibilities for the integration of the remote subsidiary's work with that of the group can also be assumed to differ with the function involved, it being easier to integrate production and purchasing in this way than R & D. Production investments aimed at taking advantage of low labour costs tend, for example, to be quite common in SEA.

This book deals with the organization of business activities in this relatively new area of TNC activities, being concerned in particular with those parts of the organization in new and remote markets that are close to customers there – for example, sales companies, manufacturing and R & D units, coordination centres, and various types of regional administrative units. An earlier study showed regional centres to be a vital part of the organization in remote areas (Jansson, 1988).

Although the nucleus of the book concerns the local organization of TNC subsidiaries in SEA, the manner in which these are related to the worldwide organization is also examined. The latter is done in two steps. First, transactions of local units with other group units are focused upon. Second, the partial within-group organization thus considered is related to the global organization of the group in question. Although the transactions involved are studied mainly from the bottom up, those in the top organization are examined as well, for example in strategic centres such as group or divisional headquarters, in part to illuminate the local organization and how it is related to the global organization.

European TNCs have extended their operations to SEA in various ways (Jansson, 1989). To understand how the organization of multinational firms develops, it is important to consider the process of establishment, in the present context that is occurring within distant markets. Research on internationalization processes in transnational corporations in general indicates such corporations to first establish themselves in geographically and culturally proximate countries and to only then proceed to more distant markets. This process is found to emerge in a stepwise manner, starting with agent arrangements and passing on from sales to manufacturing companies. Companies commit themselves through a gradual process of learning. The information and search costs, as well as perceived risks, are higher in international than in domestic investments. (Caves, 1982, pp. 68-73; Johanson and Wiedersheim-Paul, 1975; Johanson and Mattsson, 1987; Lundgren and Hedlund, 1983; Hedlund and Kverneland, 1985; Nicholas, 1986; Jansson, 1989.)

AN INSTITUTIONAL APPROACH TO TRANSNATIONAL ORGANIZATION

An institutional approach is used for illuminating local and regional organization of TNCs in remote markets and the relation of this partial organization to the overall worldwide organization. The conception of institutions emphasized here builds directly on Whitley's (1992, p. 10) definition of business systems: 'as particular arrangements of hierarchy-market relations which become institutionalized and relatively successful in particular contexts'. The particular arrangements of hierarchy-market relations are considered here in the present context as economic institutions and the specific contexts in which they are found as non-economic institutions. A transaction-cost theory is developed to explain behaviour within the economic institution of major interest in the book, the European TNC. This theory expresses very well the main rationale behind TNCs' originating from and mainly operating within Western market economies. The theory involves interpreting organizational behaviour from an economic perspective.

A major reason for utilizing transaction-cost theory in this context is that it is of an institutional character. A theory regarding corporations of the type operating in different institutional environments around the world does well to consider the institutional aspect. Indeed, this is the major way of analysing the transnational or international dimension in such a company. The large differences in institutional set-up between industrialized and LICs makes an institutional approach to multinational organizations particularly fruitful. The differentiation of subsidiary control, for example, that is achieved in such a company is assumed to depend on the mixture found of external economic and non-economic institutions. Marketing, purchasing, production, and the organization of these activities are adapted to such environments.

Another advantage of basing the study on transaction-cost theory is that this makes it possible to integrate theories of the organization of international business with theories regarding specific international business disciplines or functions, for example theories on marketing, purchasing and production. This will be developed later on in the book.

Using transaction-cost theory implies a competitive perspective. Strategies of TNCs in LICs such as those in SEA are different from those of the uninational (domestic) firms there. Generally speaking, the TNCs are technologically superior and are backed and influenced by an extremely large organization outside the host country. The strategies employed often originate outside the country and are transplanted there through the local market company. Local strategies tend to be coordinated with global strategies (Jansson, 1993). The present investigation focuses on sales companies, since they are more common and are the preferred mode of organization in the markets that were studied. So as to create a broader perspective, a comparison is made with production companies (production centres) and with agencies. In this way, the main stages of foreign involvement can be related to each other. The organization locally is also explained in light of the transnational organization of the firm. This approach seems fruitful in view of the fact that the influence of the TNC organization on competitiveness has changed within recent years.

The integration of the different activities of a TNC is of central importance today to the TNC's competitive strength. Dunning (1988a, pp. 172-3) reviews changes in the patterns of TNC activity found over the last 15 years and how these in turn have influenced ownership advantages:

1. The country-wise base has been broadened. First European TNCs, then Japanese TNCs and most recently TNCs from developing countries have become more international. The competitiveness of these companies is based on different ownership advantages than earlier TNCs had.
2. The degree of foreign involvement has grown. This has increased the advantages attaining through common governance.

As these first two points indicate, TNCs are based today in a variety of different countries. In addition, they are generally multi-product and are highly diversified geographically.

3. The forms of involvement have also been broadened. The 'new' TNCs are more willing to use other contract forms, such as joint ventures.
4. Uninational firms have become more competitive in certain industries previously dominated by TNCs.
5. Major advances in international transport, in the acquisition and interpretation of information, and in communications technology have very much facilitated international operations, making common governance easier.

An important result of these developments is that ownership advantages are increasingly based on firm-specific characteristics and less on country-specific factors. This has more to do with efficiency in reducing the transaction costs of integrative activities and what activities units have in common than with the appropriation of rents from proprietary assets for single or segmented activities. Global competition is increasingly affected by hierarchical advantages (efficiency). Dunning (1988a, p. 211) has summarized this, stating:

> We have suggested there is some reason to suppose that intra-industry production is the last stage in the evolvement of international economic transactions which begins with inter-industry trade and one-way asset transfer based on country-specific ownership advantages of single-product MNEs. Inter-industry production or intra-industry trade follows, and then finally – where there are advantages of the common governance of plants located in different countries – we get intra-industry production, based on firm-specific transaction-cost economizing advantages of multi-product MNE oligopolists from different countries.

Institutions

As already discussed, the main reason for basing the present study on transaction-cost theory is institutional, since the theory expresses well the main rationale behind TNCs originating from and mainly operating within Western market economies. This matter is elaborated upon in a quotation to be presented, which takes up how one major non-economic institution – culture – influences the economic institution of major interest here, namely the Western TNC. The quotation indicates how transaction-cost theory highlights and captures the dominant orientation, the basic beliefs, the values and behaviour, and 'soul' of this Western market-oriented economic institution.

> As the Western culture derives its main orientations from the Judeo-Christian or Greco-Hellinist traditions, order, symmetry, linearity, and individuality are the bases of an epistemological framework. Organisations are the systemic hierarchy of individual parts. As such, their efficiency and efficacy can be analysed down to the smallest unit i.e. individual. The unit's individual outcomes can be aggregated to obtain the results of the whole outcomes. As the organisation compares and contrasts the efficacy of different units, the systematic allocation of resources among them becomes of prime concern. In fact, the Western economic concept is mainly built on allocation of resources or allocative efficiency. On the other hand, if organisations are regarded as symbiotic relations of heterogeneous parts mutually benefiting all concerned, the precise demarcation of contributions is not possible and will not be attempted. Instead, measurement will be based more on the totality of the system than on individual parts. The results of these divergent views can be observed in the ways the American and Japanese organisations

measure their efficiency results. The American organisation, the prototype of the developed system in the West, emphasises decentralisation and individual unit measurement.

The wave of decentralisation unit and accountability (sic) that had overtaken American businesses in the seventies is indicative of how the concept of allocative efficiency has carried itself to its logical extreme. On the other hand, Japanese companies are always looking for the contributions of synergetic relationships, because synergy is considered the basis of organisational relations. Thus, American firms will look for precise measurements of each sub-unit's performance in the shorter term, while Japanese firms are interested in fostering systems of relationships that will contribute to synergetic results. Thus, they will be more concerned with overall and long-term effects rather than with short-term and individual results. They are willing to tolerate the organisational units which may be inefficient by themselves but may produce positive effects in relation to others. In fact, the whole Japanese approach is aimed at the totality rather than the parts. The Japanese industrial system – Miti and the whole complex of individual companies – is aiming for total efficiency rather than their individual unit profits.

That is the difference which makes the Japanese organisation so formidable. Though this approach is clearly seen in the Japanese companies and culture, other Asian cultures share the totality concept in varying degrees. (Khin, 1988, pp. 217-18)

Differences in institutional environments thus lead to differences in types of economic institutions or organizational forms. According to Whitley (1992, p. 14) research shows that compared with Eastern Asian firms Western firms

> ... share a common reliance on legal-rational norms and bases of legitimacy. Similarly, the prevalence of capital market-based financial systems, and the reliance on 'professional' modes of skill development and organization, in Anglo-Saxon societies means that dominant businesses in Britain and the USA seem to share a preference for financial means of control of operations and subsidiaries, and accord the finance function higher status than many continental European firms.

As Whitley emphasizes, the financial system in the UK is less credit-based than the financial systems in the rest of Western Europe. The types of control exerted by TNCs from different Western countries thus vary, a matter to be considered further in Chapter 2, where the TNC is discussed as an economic institution. However, the commonalities of Western European TNCs are stressed in this book and not the differences. These various corporations share a wide variety of institutions, for example market-based wage systems, professionally-oriented occupations and commitments to individualism, which together result in characteristics common to such economic institutions as the TNC. This type of institution belongs to a broader institutional category known as the 'corporation', which is one of six basic institutions which Sjöstrand (1985, 1992) discusses. A corporation, or a TNC, is a rationality type context for human exchange. It involves a calculative interaction rationale and a hierarchic form of interaction.

> ... 'modern society's division of work, specialization and benefits from scale economics create a strong dependence on unknown others. This uncertainty about the actions of the many anonymous others, who ultimately decide the wealth and survival of each individual, was previously often reduced or absorbed by the status system, i.e., by social positions like those of the family, clan, neighbours, and friends. Such (dependent) relations and their accompanying interactions are here denominated "genuine" relationships. This way of reducing uncertainty – by relating to known others – is still most relevant, but at least during this century, it has been attenuated by other forms such as common values and – most significantly – calculative behaviour. Both the latter forms refer to dependence on unknown others, which is significant in the modern industrialized society. (Sjöstrand, 1992, p. 1017)

The main economic logic in such an economic institution can be expressed in terms of transaction-cost theories. Transaction costs occur in transactions between economic units, within the market or within the firm.

Institutional economics is a fruitful approach here, since in these terms economics is not viewed as a universal science in which economic models can be used out of context. The neoclassical tradition, in contrast, is founded on the principle of universality, a principle which institutional economists repudiate. Myrdal (1968), for example, stresses the importance of the broader societal context for an understanding of economic behaviour in developing countries. Williamson (1985) discusses certain economic institutions and various economic forms of organizing behaviour that provide an important basis for the present study. However, in terms of the theory he propounds, the state is largely limited to its purely legal role. The economic institutions Williamson develops are therefore complemented by, and broadly related to, various non-economic institutions. The approach taken here is based on the assumption that economic behaviour follows an efficiency logic expressed mainly in the various governance forms, such behaviour being viewed in a broader institutional context, than for example of the culture or of the nation or state.

As the author indicated earlier (Jansson, 1993), a consequence of the institutional approach is that, in analysing industrial marketing, one considers systemic functions and institutions and not simply dyadic exchanges. These involve transaction processes that are supported by economic, legal, and other institutions. The major goal of a firm is to reduce transaction-costs so as to achieve an efficient exchange of resources for a given industrial need. Different characteristics of the transactions provide the conditions needed for a particular economic institution to be organized efficiently. Inversely, economic institutions vary in their ability to organize different types of transactions. They set boundaries to transactions.

Economic institutions are thus confined in turn, by other, non-economic institutional frameworks. As already discussed, the common values and attitudes within a society, which represent a non-economic institution, may either facilitate or obstruct the formation of a more specialized economic institution such as that of the TNC, which is calculative in nature and is oriented towards efficiency. The legal framework is another such basic institution. The costs related to these non-economic institutions are normally not included in transaction cost analysis, for example costs for creating laws, common values, and other types of infrastructure in order to achieve efficient transactions in society. Instead, they constitute conditions basic to and prerequisite for, efficient economic transactions. As was indicated, these basic institutions found in LICs cannot be taken for granted in LICs and left out of the analysis, especially since the external costs they involve may need to be internalized by the parties. In the present context, both non-economic and economic institutions are considered as influencing transaction costs. Since transaction costs are defined from the perspective of the business units involved, a deficient or not particularly appropriate aspect of a non-economic institution such as the legal system can be said to increase transaction costs for the concerned parties, for example through producing a high degree of uncertainty. The costs of establishing and running such institutions are normally borne in Western Europe by the state, at the same time as they represent public property. In certain Asian countries, in contrast, they may be internalized by individual economic agents so as to become private property.

PREVIOUS RESEARCH ON THE TRANSNATIONAL CORPORATION

The theoretical framework developed in this book draws on recent research concerning TNCs and subsidiaries, research centred on transaction costs.

Research at the Subsidiary Level

Recent research on complex TNCs indicates the degree of control a TNC has over its subsidiaries to vary markedly from one subsidiary to another, affecting for example the strategic role and strategic context of the subsidiary (Bartlett, 1986; Bartlett and Ghoshal, 1989; Forsgren and Holm, 1991; Ghoshal and Nohria, 1989; Gupta and Govindarajan, 1991; Hedlund, 1986; Martinez and Jarillo, 1991; Porter, 1986). This has mainly been established by studying large subsidiaries at strategic locations within the inner core of TNCs. On the basis of such research, it can be hypothesized that the relatively small subsidiaries in SEA taken up in this book, which occupy a position at the periphery of the group, are controlled differently from large subsidiaries in Europe and North America.

Studies of TNCs at the individual subsidiary level tend to overplay the importance of informal organization at the expense of formal organization structures in explaining subsidiary behaviour (e.g. Martinez and Jarillo, 1991; Gupta and Govindarajan, 1991). Various studies have shown, nevertheless, that organizational variables and internal management processes change more frequently and to a greater extent than formal structures (e.g. Bartlett and Ghoshal, 1989; Prahalad and Doz, 1987). However, the research on which such conclusions are based can in turn be seen as representing a reaction to earlier studies, based on Chandler's strategy-structure perspective, which tended to overemphasize structure (e.g. Stopford and Wells, 1972; Franko, 1976). The formal organizational structure should indeed be regarded as providing an important means of control of the actions of subsidiaries. To examine the matter further, finer graded formal macrostructures should be developed so as to allow greater insight to be obtained into how different types of subsidiaries are controlled. Both formal structure and internal management processes should be regarded as important. This is a basic assumption of the present study with its institutional perspective and its inclusion of external institutions as contingency elements.

Transaction-cost Based Research

A transaction-cost theory can be seen as highly useful in the insight it provides into the functioning of the TNC. The theory takes a very broad view of organizations and treats the transaction as the basic unit of organizational activity. A transaction event or transaction process is regarded as organized if it exhibits regular patterns and structures (Barney and Ouchi, 1986). In contrast to organization theory, and to interorganizational theory as well, transaction-cost theory does not take the organization for granted, its thus being a more basic theory, one focusing on organizational boundaries.

An institutional approach, in turn, provides considerable insight into contingency elements in the TNC organization's functioning through relating internal organizational aspects to the type or types of external organization found. This is a main departure from the tradition of viewing the TNC as a unitary organization operating in a simplified environment. Such an institutional approach to the multinational organization is similar in many ways to a network approach, for example one which attempts to integrate the organizational network within the TNC with networks that are external to it. Ghoshal and Bartlett (1990), in their major treatise on the network approach to the organization of TNCs recently, stress the advantages of such an approach (see also Forsgren and Pahlberg, 1991; Forsgren and Holm, 1991; Jansson, Sharma and Saqib, 1993).

Transaction-cost theory is particularly useful in studying high-technology industries, something particularly applicable here. Buckley (1988b, p. 131) notes the following:

> Contributions by Casson (1985), Teece (1983), Buckley (1987), Nicholas (1986) and others have shown that the incidence of transactions costs is particularly high in vertically integrated process industries, knowledge-intensive industries, quality-assurance dependent products and communication-intensive industries.

The form of transaction-cost theory presented in this book reflects two main lines of theoretical development, namely that of the theory of multinational enterprise, in which transaction-cost explanations play a prominant role today, and the branch of transaction-cost theory that governance forms represent (Williamson, 1979, 1981, 1985). In the former case, the analysis of the transnational corporation in the present book is based mainly on the eclectic paradigm (Dunning, 1981, 1988a,b), and to some degree on the internalization theory of the multinational firm (Buckley and Casson, 1976; Buckley, 1987; Casson, 1987; Rugman, 1981) and on ideas stemming from closely related research (Hennart, 1982; Caves, 1982; Teece, 1986).

These two major theories cannot be used directly, however, since they deal with organizational modes in only a general way and do not concern to any extent the organization of the modes themselves. Dunning (1988a, pp. 175-77) makes a useful distinction between three main efficiency-based theories for analysing the determinants of the organizational modes of international involvement. The first is the theory of internalization, developed to explain the growth of multinational firms. In terms of this theory, a TNC represents a 'market failure' as such, although it possesses an efficient internal market. This is a purely economic theory, employing marginal analysis as its basic approach. Dunning (1988a, p. 177) concludes:

> In particular, the authors concentrate on the conditions in which firms choose to internalize international markets for technology information and certain types of raw materials, and for manufactured goods and services where product quality and reliability are particularly important selling strengths.

The second efficiency-based theory is appropriability theory, which focuses on how a TNC can best appropriate the economic rent from its proprietary assets (Magee, 1977), and is not applicable to the organization theory developed in this book. The main question considered by that theory is the type of economic organization providing the firm with the highest return.

These two efficiency-based theories have a common drawback in terms of the organizational focus of this book, namely that they serve to explain the degree of multinationalism attained rather than the functioning of the multinational organization as such. This is a conclusion that Calvet (1980, pp. 174-75) summarized very well.

> ... an eclectic approach implies that trade theory, location theory, industrial organization theory and property rights theory all have something to contribute to an explanation of why firms decide to transact with foreign countries. To these must be added a hierarchies vs markets theory, to account for the choice of transaction mode.
> Multinationalism = f(T1, T2, T3, T4)
> In other words, the extent of multinationalism is determined by variables pertaining to trade theory (T1), location theory (T2), industrial organization theory (T3), and property rights theory (T4). One would also expect that the higher the cost differentials, the higher the advantages to be gained from multiple locations, the more R and D or advertising expenditures, the stronger the patent protection or the monopolistic returns of firms, the more important the degree of multinationalism would be. In turn, Hierarchical multinationalism = f (T5) where T5 refers to the markets vs hierarchies theory.

This book draws mainly on this markets and hierarchies theory or governance forms theory, which is the third efficiency-based theory that Dunning refers to. The governance forms theory differs most markedly from the other theories referred to above in being an institutional theory, or a new-institutional theory as it is usually called.

This theory concerns the nature of a firm's transactions and evaluates the relative costs of organizing these in terms of four different governance forms: market, bilateral, trilateral, and unified governance. Unified governance concerns the internal organization of transactions through a hierarchy, whereas the others concern the external organization of transactions.

As Buckley (1988b, p. 130) indicates, the governance forms theory has a marked legal bias. In this book, however, the theory is extended from its more usual use as a means of analysing the TNC in terms of its being a legal organization to that of analysing the TNC viewed as a managerial organization.

Since the TNC is considered in the present context as a means of organizing transactions, how it is organized as an economic institution as seen from the perspective of transaction costs needs to be analysed in depth. This is done in Chapter 2.

THE ASEAN COUNTRIES

The organization of a TNC in East Asia is influenced by specific changes which occur there in the region external to the firm. The main reason for the TNCs that were studied doing business in SEA is the rapid economic development there and the profitable markets this creates. The high rate of growth encompasses many new industries and large investments in infrastructure, which lead to the demand for many types of industrial products. This high demand represents one of four major reasons for the substantial number of foreign investments in SEA, one especially important to the European TNCs. The rapid economic development which has occurred has also created an increasingly affluent population that demands cars and household appliances and many other consumer products. A second reason for such investments is that most of the countries are rich in resources and have received considerable investments of a supply-oriented character, mainly from Japan and the USA. The third reason is the advantageousness of locating production facilities in SEA so as to benefit from the low wages and the efficient labour force. As will be indicated in Chapter 4, this factor has no particular weight for the TNCs that were studied, since they are not very active in the electronics industry or in other industries, in which labour-intensive production operations are common. The fourth reason for investment in the region is one important to many of the TNCs that were studied.

For these firms, investments in SEA are based on more than simply the local or regional advantages, but rather are also reflective of their desire to increase their global competitiveness in relation to various Asian firms, primarily those from Japan. The idea is that by competing in Asia the competitiveness of these Asian corporations in Europe and North America can be reduced somewhat.

There are large differences between the various countries of the region, regarding such characteristics as area, population, general structure of the economy, industrial structure, and the like. This can be seen in the profiles of the five main ASEAN countries presented in Table 1.1. As can be seen, Singapore is the most industrialized country, with the highest percentage of its work force in manufacturing, and with the highest per capita income. It is followed, as regards these aspects, by Malaysia and Thailand, which in turn are followed by Indonesia and the Philippines. Another sign of the special position of Singapore is that it is the only newly industrialized country (NIC) in the area having an economic structure highly skewed to the manufacturing and service industries. Malaysia is also close to achieving this status, due to its high involvement in the manufacturing industry in relation to the total value added, a category of industry which is neither low-tech nor driven by labour costs. Thailand is also rapidly leaving its former level of industrialization and is approaching NIC-status, whereas Indonesia and the Philippines, in contrast, are far from this goal. The manufacturing industry of these latter two countries is low-tech and competes on the basis of its low wages, primarily with China and Vietnam, which are quickly approaching them. The export-oriented policies of development of all the five major ASEAN countries, which result in a high dependence of these countries on foreign trade and foreign markets, are clearly evident in the figures presented in Table 1.1. During recent years there has been a considerable shift away from markets in the US and Europe to Asian markets, something which can be clearly seen in the table.

This increasing economic integration within the region represents a very profound change. SEA is rapidly becoming more homogeneous. With the establishment of the ASEAN Free Trade Area (AFTA), the countries of Brunei, Indonesia, Malaysia, Philippines, Singapore and Thailand are all prepared for greater economic integration. In certain regions within this large economic block, integration is occurring rapidly, for example in the economic growth 'triangle' that links Singapore with the Malaysian state of Johor and this in turn with Indonesia's Riau Islands. The opening up of Vietnam to foreign direct

Table 1.1 Performance figures for five ASEAN countries

	Indo-nesia	Malay-sia	Philip-pines	Singa-pore	Thai-land
Area ('000 km^2)	1,948	329.8	300	0.6	513
Population					
Total	185	18.6	60.7	2.8	57.6
Projected year 2010 (m)	275	27	76.5	3.2	75.8
Urban pop. as % of total	31	60	48.4	100	27
Life expectancy (years)	61	70,74(F)	65	75-77	65
Workforce					
% manufacturing	10.7	20.1	9.5	28.2	17
% agriculture/fishing	48.5	26.8	41.3	0.2	57
Social					
Telephones ('000)	3,230	2,100	889	1,080	1,900
Cars ('000)	1,700	1,800	453	285	2,300
Trucks and commercial vehicles ('000)	1,785	201	846	120.8	614
Length of railways ('000 km)	4.23	2.00	1.20	n.a.	3.80
Length of paved highway ('000 km)	5.24	46.89	160.63	2.9	46.00
Production					
GDP at market prices (US$ b) '91	116.16	93.26	45.12	43.17	92.0
Per capita income (US$) '91	638	2,448	n.a	11,845	1,604
GDP, real growth '91 (%)	6.8	8.8	-0.9	6.7	7.5
% avg. GDP growth '87-'91	n.a.	8.3	3.8	n.a.	10.4
Manufacturing as % GDP	n.a.	30.0	25.5	17.4	26.1
Agriculture as % GDP	n.a.	16.0	21.3	0.2	12.4
Foreign trade					
Merchandise exports (US$m) 1991	29,142	34,440	8,840	61,300	28,407
% manufacturers	51.7	64.1	81.0	59.0	65.4
% food and farm products	7.8	13.2	15.4	2.2	26.9
% metals and minerals	23.7	15.1	3.5	n.a.	1.0
% export growth 1992[1]	6.6	10.7	8.1	0.4	16.0
Merchandise imports (US$m) 1991	25,869	37,380	12,051	66,000	38,114
% plant, capital equipment	29.7	41.7	24.5	46.0	40.3
Foreign trade as % GDP	n.a.	n.a.	46.3	294.0	72.3
% import growth 1992[1]	4.7	5.0	8.7	0.5	6.0
% trade with Pacific region (excluding US and Japan)	34.5	36.0	30.4	47.0	25.9
% trade with Japan	37.0	21.4	19.7	15.3	24.5
% trade with US	12.0	16.1	26.3	14.6	15.2
Current-account balance (US$m) 1991	72,901	-4,300	-1,033	4,200	-7,820
Public debt-service ratio (%)	25.4	6.4	8.6	n.a.	11.0
Education as % budget	5.4	3.7	12.3	14.7	19.2
Annual inflation 1992[1] (%)	24.0	4.6	8.9	2.4	4.5
Unemployment rate 1992[1] (%)	n.a.	4.1	11.0	1.9	4.6

[1] = Estimates by a panel of economists

Sources: Asia 1993 Yearbook, pp. 6-9; *Far Eastern Economic Review*, 24-31 December. 1992, p. 58.

investment (FDI), and probably of Laos and Cambodia as well in the future, may give these countries closer ties with AFTA, mainly through the mediation of Thailand. The freeing of China's economy has increased the FDI in that country tremendously, mainly by companies from Japan, Hong Kong and Taiwan, which has created a new economic block in Northeast Asia. Since these countries, along with South Korea, are also the main investors in Southeast Asia and plan to increase their investments there even more in the years to come, the economic integration of Eastern Asia is growing rapidly. In 1992, for example, 40% of the trade of these countries took place within the area. Cooperation between East Asian countries, Australia, New Zealand, the USA and Canada is also emerging rapidly, furthered by the Asia-Pacific Economic Caucus (APEC).

These forces of integration, together with the rapid economic growth of the area, have a profound effect on the organization of the European TNCs located there. The regional organization in SEA is growing in importance. Singapore is the prime centre of regional activity there now, but Bangkok will surely begin to become more competitive if economic growth in Indo-China takes off. The regional organization in Northeast Asia is also becoming more important. Hong Kong and Tokyo are the traditional centres of regional activity there, but Taipeh is becoming of increasing interest as a gateway to China through Taiwan's heavy investments in Southern China. With the increasing integration of Eastern Asia, the creation of a single regional centre encompassing or drawing together the whole area is an increasing possibility.

The policies of development established in SEA (exclusive of the Philippines) and in many other parts of Eastern Asia combine economic freedom with political autocracy. This has led to a modern Western-influenced economic sector coexisting with a traditional political sector. The meeting of these two sectors often results in corruption, which is a part of life in many ASEAN countries, and a difficult issue for many foreign firms to handle (Jansson, 1993). Corruption seems to be particularly common in the conducting of business with government units. As a result of this situation, efforts are frequently made, particularly by domestic companies, to gain commercial advantage through political patronage. However, such a meeting of sectors is also positive for economic development, since governments play an important role in the high rate of economic growth. The states here are highly managed market economies, a governance clearly reminiscent of that found in the modern TNC which is controlled by a combination of prices (markets) and administrative directives (autocracy). The degree and type of government control varies between the different countries and sectors. Such control is more direct and the degree of regulation greater in Indonesia, the Philippines and Malaysia, as compared with the more indirect control and lesser degree of regulation in Singapore. The mixing of economy and politics has created tensions in society, something which could risk the continued rapid growth in the area. There are signs of change in this respect, due to an increasing trend toward political liberalization, although this may be too slow and the results too late in coming.

Being situated at one of the main crossways of the world, the area is strong in foreign influence, although this differs between the countries. The English influence is still felt in the former English colonies of Singapore and Malaysia, the Dutch influence in Indonesia and the Spanish and the later American impact in the Philippines. In Thailand, which never was colonized, the influence is broader and of a more general character. The strong Japanese impact on the area is more recent. Religion, which came to the region via the trade routes, varies between countries. The Malays, found in Indonesia and Malaysia, are Muslims, the Thais are Buddhists, whereas the Filipinos are Roman Catholics. Singapore does not have any official religion, but most Chinese there are either Confucianists, Taoists, Buddhists or a combination of these.

Besides contributing to the variegated nature of the area, culture is also a homogenizing factor, particularly in business, which is dominated by about 20 million overseas Chinese, who have come here from mainly Southern China. Therefore, the organization of European TNCs cannot be adequately understood unless account is also taken of the characteristics of the Chinese business system.

THE TNCs STUDIED

In this section a brief summary is provided of the subsidiaries that were studied and the groups to which they belong. As can be seen in Table 1.2, most of the TNCs in question are well-represented in all of the five major ASEAN countries (Brunei being excluded), their operations in SEA constituting a 'natural' part of their worldwide operations. Thirteen of them are very large multinational firms active in most parts of the world, and the majority of them appear on the

Table 1.2 The representation of the TNCs studied in SEA (1991)

	ASEAN Singa- pore	Malay- sia	Thai- land	Indo- nesia	Philip- pines	Rest of Asia
Pacmat	PC(RO)*	SC	SC*	A	SC	SA+EA
Wear and Tear	SC+*	A	A			EA
Paving systems	SC+*	A	A	A	A	PA
Food equipment	RO*;SC*	SC*	SC*	A,PC	A	
Telecom	RO*;A	SC2*;PC	SC	A	A	
Indpow87	RO*;SC*	PC*;SC*	PC*;SC*	A	PC	
Conmine	SC(RO)*	SC*	A	SC, D	SC	
Tooltec	RC+*	SC*	SC	D	SC	EA
Weldprod	RO*;SC*	SC	A	PC;A	A	EA
Explo	A	PC(RO)*	A	A	PC	
Indcomp	RO+*;SC; PC	SC,PC	D	D	D	PA
Drives	SC*	SC	A	A	A	
Specmat	RO*;SC	SC	SC	D	D	PA
Homeprod	SC*	SC*,PC	SC	A	SC, PC	
Match87		PC*	PC		RO+;PC	SA+EA
Trans	RO+*, D	PC*, D	PC*,D	PC, D	D	EA
Pills	RO+*,SC	SC	SC	D	SC	EA

Abbreviations:

PA = The Pacific-Asia basin except USA; SA = South Asia; EA = East Asia;
A = Agent; SC = Sales company; PC = Production company; D = Distributor; RC = Regional company; RO = Regional office.
* = Companies interviewed
+ = The regional organization covers a larger area than does the ASEAN, results which are shown in the right-hand column
2 = The number of companies
87 = These TNCs were only studied between 1984 and 1987.

Fortune 500 list. As can be seen in Table 1.3, one of the firms, *Paving Systems*, has only minor activity in ASEAN. Four of the TNCs (*Wear and Tear, Explo, Drives, and Specmat*) have a high degree of internationalization but are considerably smaller than the major TNCs that were studied. *Wear and Tear* differs from the others in being a fairly small but rather highly internationalized TNC with only limited operations in SEA. This TNC is owned by a holding company that possesses a very diverse portfolio of companies.

All the TNCs that were studied are industrial companies operating in hi-tech industries, 13 of them mainly selling their products to other manufacturers. The main industrial products the companies sell in SEA are listed in Table 1.4, the major customer industries being dealt with in Table 1.5. As can be seen in the tables, three of the TNCs (*Homeprod, Match, and Trans*) sell mainly consumer products and one of the TNCs (*Pills*) concentrates on the sale of drugs, primarily to professional organizations. As one can also note (see Jansson, 1993 for more details), most of the 13 TNCs that sell goods to producers offer a wide variety of these goods to many different types of industries in ASEAN. However, there are also a few TNCs which concentrate on only a few main products. As noted above, three TNCs sell consumer products, two of them shopping goods. Of these two, one (*Homeprod*) sells home appliances, and one (*Trans*) sells vehicles, the latter company also selling to other firms and to institutional buyers. The third company concentrates on one main type of convenience good (*Match*).

As will be dealt with further in Chapter 4, the TNCs have gradually established themselves in SEA. Some started rather early, but the major growth took place from about the end of the 1970s onwards. The way the TNCs are organized varies a great deal. The global organization of the groups is considered in Chapter 3. Local organizational aspects within SEA are taken up mainly in Chapters 5 and 6.

In an earlier book (Jansson, 1993) the industrial marketing strategies of the TNCs in question were considered in detail. The marketing behaviour of these firms is dealt with briefly here too, in the second part of Chapter 4. Compared with marketing, manufacturing is only carried out in the ASEAN countries by these TNCs to a limited degree. As will become evident in Chapter 4, production there is nevertheless important for seven of the firms and is much less important for three of them, whereas the remaining seven have no production in the region at all. With a few exceptions, the typical production problems of TNC subsidiaries located in LICs, problems

Table 1.3 Profiles of the TNCs studied (1990)

NAME	Pacmat	Wear & Tear	Paving systems	Food equip	Tele-com	Ind-pow	Conmine
GROUP ORGANIZATION							
No. of business areas/ divisions	F	-/2	8/-	7/-	6/-	8/65	3/7
No. of companies	-	10	300	-	150	1300	50
East Asia	-	1	9	6	13	-	10
Southeast Asia	4	1	5	3	8	-	3
SALES							
Total (in US$ billion)	5	0.1	1.6	5.6	9	25	3
Europe (%)	55	-	80	53	60	57	54
East Asia (%)	3	-	9[1]	7	6	15[2]	9
Southeast Asia (%)	-	1.5	-	2	-	-	-
EMPLOYEES							
Total (thousands)	12	1	25	21	70	141	21
Europe (%)	-	-	95	70	80	65	56
East Asia (%)	-	1.5	0.2	3.5	4[1]	9	12
Southeast Asia (%)	-	1.5	0.07	1.7	-	-	-
PRODUCTION							
East Asia	Yes	No	Yes	Yes	Yes	Yes	Yes
Southeast Asia	Yes	No	Yes	No	Yes	No	No

NAME	Tool-tec	Weld-prod	Explo	Ind-comp	Dri-ves	Spec-mat
GROUP ORGANIZATION						
No. of business areas/ divisions	6/-	4/-	F	5/-	4/-	F
No. of companies	-	48	-	180	40	55
East Asia	10	5	-	17	3	8
Southeast Asia	4	3	2	9	2	4
SALES						
Total (in US$ billion)	3.6	1	-	5.6	0.5	0.5
Europe (%)	60	60	-	63	-	-
East Asia (%)	-	-	-	-	-	-
Southeast Asia (%)	-	-	-	-	-	-
EMPLOYEES						
Total (thousands)	26	8	-	49	4	3.5
Europe (%)	70	42	-	75	83	80
East Asia (%)	3.5	5	-	1.6	3	7
Southeast Asia (%)	0.6	1	-	1	0.5	3
PRODUCTION						
East Asia	Yes	No	Yes	Yes	No	No
Southeast Asia	Yes	No	Yes	Yes	No	No

NAME	Home-prod	Match[3]	Trans	Pills
GROUP ORGANIZATION				
No. of business areas/ divisions	5/19	3/-	4/-	F/Regional
No. of companies	600	150	73	40
East Asia	7	6	7	8
Southeast Asia	3	6	5	4
SALES				
Total (in US$ billion)	16	3	16	2
Europe (%)	65	75	62	65
East Asia (%)	4	3	10	11
Southeast Asia (%)	0.7	3	-	2
EMPLOYEES				
Total (thousands)	151	34	69	9
Europe (%)	43	55	85	65
East Asia (%)	9	6	3	10
Southeast Asia (%)	5	6	-	6
PRODUCTION				
East Asia	Yes	Yes	Yes	Yes
Southeast Asia	Yes	Yes	Yes	Yes

1 = Includes the whole of Asia; 2 = + Australia/New Zealand; 3 = The profile of this TNC is from 1987; F = Functional organization.

based on import-substitution policies, are not that germane in SEA. Supplier development, for instance, has only been forced upon two of the TNCs. Most of the TNCs are allowed to import what they need rather freely.

This can be seen as no more than a short introduction to the TNCs of interest here. The operations of these companies will be illustrated and analysed in the chapters that follow. The reader will thus learn more about the companies bit by bit as their various activities are dealt with. The aim will not be, however, to provide a full account of the organization of each and every company. Rather common patterns among them are described. In addition, only those companies with aspects particularly well suited to illustrate the points of interest will be taken up in the different chapters.

Table 1.4 Main groups of products sold in SEA by the TNCs studied

Product group	TNC
INDUSTRIAL PRODUCTS	
1. Raw materials (RM)	
2. Processed materials (PE)	Pacmat, Tooltec, Specmat
3. Castings and forgings (CF)	
4. Components and subassemblies (COM)	Indpow, Wear and Tear, Food equipment, Indcomp
5. Minor equipment (MIE)	Indpow, Weldprod, Food equipment, Tooltec, Conmine, Drives
6. Major equipment (MJE)	Indpow, Telecom, Pacmat, Paving systems, Conmine, Food equipment, Weldprod
7. Maintenance, repair and operating items (MRO)	Indpow, Explo, Wear and Tear, Food equipment, Tooltec, Conmine, Indcomp
CONSUMER PRODUCTS	
8. Convenience goods	Match
9. Shopping goods	Homeprod, Trans
10. Drugs	Pills

METHODOLOGY

The methodology employed in the research project on which this book is based is described in detail elsewhere, most comprehensively in Jansson (1993). In this section, therefore, only a few general remarks regarding methodology will be made.

Theory Development

A theoretical framework based on an institutional approach and on transaction-cost theory has been developed for an organizational

Table 1.5 Main customer industries

INDUSTRIAL PRODUCTS	
INFRASTRUCTURE	
Construction	Conmine, Indpow, Explo, Wear and Tear
Roads, railways etc.	Indpow, Conmine, Explo Paving systems, Weldprod
Telecommunications	Telecom
BASIC INDUSTRY	
Power	Indpow, Conmine, Food equipment
Steel	Food equipment, Drives
Shipping, off-shore	Indpow, Food equipment, Drives Weldprod, Conmine
Oil	Tooltec, Drives
Mining	Conmine, Wear and Tear, Drives
Petrochemicals	Food equipment, Tooltec, Drives
ENGINEERING INDUSTRY	
Machinery	Tooltec, Indpow, Specmat
Electronics	Indpow, Conmine, Specmat
Packaging	Pacmat, Food equipment
General	Conmine, Indpow, Indcomp, Tooltec, Specmat
FOOD INDUSTRY	Food equipment, Drives
TEXTILE INDUSTRY	Indcomp, Tooltec
CERAMIC INDUSTRY	Wear and Tear
FOREST INDUSTRY	Tooltec
CONSUMER PRODUCTS	
HOME APPLIANCES	Homeprod
MATCHES	Match
DRUGS	Pills
TRANSPORT EQUIPMENT	Trans

analysis of the TNCs in which sales or market companies are of special interest. These are TNCs having organizations at the border between an internal and an external organizational form. The decision to establish or to extend a hierarchical firm encompassing SEA or parts of it is taken with the sales company, whereas the decision to establish a production unit there is more of a multi-plant investment decision, one related to an earlier market investment (Nicholas, 1986). Such decisions are in accordance with an internationalization process.

An institutional approach to analysing a TNC organization has hardly been attempted previously. According to such a perspective, the subsidiary organization and the global organization are strongly dependent upon the economic institutions or governance forms that are found, or which apply. Such economic institutions are in turn constrained by non-economic institutions, for example government, the legal system, the culture, and various professional structures. Thus, non-economic institutions are assumed to be important in an institutional theory of this sort.

The institutions of a highly specific and many-faceted environment are best researched in a multi-dimensional study. The approach used here represents a combination of inductive and deductive methods, and involves a constant interchange between data and theory (Bulmer, 1979). Such an approach is not purely deductive, since it does not involve validating theories by testing hypotheses. Neither is it purely inductive. Theory here is not entirely developed from, or 'grounded' on, empirical data (Glaser and Strauss, 1967; Glaser, 1978).

Transaction-cost theory is a neoclassical institutional-economic theory dealing with general economic behaviour at high levels of abstraction. The nucleus of a business analysis, the company, is hardly present at all. In most versions, the firm is one type of contract among several, others being, for example, the principal-agent type contract or a contract founded on property rights. In one type of transaction-cost theory, governance-forms theory (Williamson, 1975, 1979, 1981, 1985), the firm is more fully developed in terms of its being an organization, and being viewed as an institution characterized by a certain organizational structure. This governance-forms theory also relates internal and external institutions to one another. However, such a transaction-cost theory cannot be used for describing and explaining organizational behaviour in a TNC directly.

A theoretical framework has been developed for the special organizational problems found within the TNCs that were studied. The framework involves a number of separate theories that are fitted to one other within an overall theoretical framework and approach, one which is a combination of an institutional approach and of transaction-cost theory. The individual theories, in turn, are ones selected from a greater number of partly relevant theories, examined for their applicability to the type of circumstances at hand. In this way they are in a sense generalized, since the end result is a theoretical framework consisting of a new combination of theories developed for a particular type of empirical situation and within the framework of a certain overall theoretical approach. This framework can then be utilized as a vehicle for examining other cases, that is, be generalized to other situations. As a consequence, a contribution can thus be made to the theory of the multinational firm, both as regards the organization of TNCs, and as regards a more general theory of the multinational enterprise. This is accomplished by applying at the organizational level a general theory of TNCs, one based on transaction costs, and transforming it into an organization theory.

Case-study Research

With the framework of the institutional perspective thus taken, the case-study method became the logical research strategy for the research project. Case studies are also preferable when analytical generalization is the main aim of the research. 'In analytical generalization, the investigator is striving to generalize a particular set of results to some broader theory.' (Yin 1984/89, p. 39). Research here does not involve statistical generalization, i.e. generalizing from samples to a universe. Rather, analytical generalization is achieved through a replication process, the relevance of various theories being studied for a variety of different cases. The purpose of the analytical generalization here is not to validate theories but to study their suitability in unfamiliar economic environments. The generalization criterion is thus replaced by a flexibility criterion (Brunsson, 1982; Bulmer, 1979).

A comparative case, or multiple case-study method is used, the cases being TNCs having local and regional companies located in SEA. Most of the data and background information were collected through interviewing. Questionnaires based on preliminary theoretical frameworks containing open-ended and non-standardized questions were used. The controls summarized in Figure 2, for example, represent important theoretical constructs that were developed in an analysis carried out during the earlier part of the project, one based both on the literature and on empirical findings, and serving as an important source of question formulation during the last round of interviews carried out, in 1991. Most of the interviews took place at the subsidiary level in SEA, having been carried out on four main occasions, involving visits there in 1984, 1985 and 1989, as well as a one-year stay in 1991. The activities of 28 subsidiaries belonging to 17 European TNCs were studied in this way between 1984 and 1991.

OUTLINE OF THE BOOK

The book consists of two main parts, the first being a purely theoretical part of one chapter, in which the TNC is described as being an economic institution (Chapter 2). The second part, consisting of the remaining chapters, is empirically based. Chapter 3 takes up the global organization of the TNCs that were studied, whereas Chapter 4 analyses, in its first section, how the local and regional organizations in SEA were built up, and how the major external transactions are organized. This latter aspect is considered in greater depth in two further sections of that chapter, which concern the organization of purchasing and production within the subsidiaries of the TNCs in the region and how the external and internal organization of the TNCs are bridged by the governing of transfer prices. The chapter provides a thorough background to the specific organizational issues present in Asia and how these subsidiaries are managed and controlled by the groups in Europe. Such organizational issues are taken up in still greater detail in Chapters 5 and 6. There the local and regional organizations of the TNCs are discussed and the question of how these types of organization are related to the global organizational form found in the respective groups is analysed.

Individual case studies will not be presented in any detail. They served, however, as the empirical basis for cross-case analysis which resulted in the theoretical framework. The book thus synthesizes the information of relevance found in the cases. The presentation of case material which is made is organized around the main theoretical topics of interest. For each topic dealt with in a chapter, a synthesis is provided of what analysis of the case material indicated. Appropriate examples are drawn from the cases to illustrate specific aspects of the topic in question.

In accordance with the conditions stipulated for the interviews, each of the case studies as a whole, as well as its informants, remain anonymous. Illustrations of specific points are provided from such case material, however, throughout the book. It is important to stress the difference between how the cases were used for developing the theories and how they are used in the book to illustrate various points. The general theoretical patterns described are based on the entire data base of case material, whereas only certain portions of the material contained in the cases are taken up in the book, with the aim here of illustrating certain aspects of the theories that were developed.

CONCLUSIONS

This book focuses on the local organization of TNCs in SEA and presents a related theoretical framework which takes the theory of the multinational firm and organization theory as its starting point. In the form in which they had been presented originally, these theories were not found to provide an adequate account of the organizational forms the subsidiaries of the TNCs had within SEA and of how the organization of the subsidiaries was related to the global organization of the respective TNCs. The development of theory here involved adopting an institutional orientation and creating an institutional theory of the TNC. In the process, a more general contribution is also made to theories applying to this basic area.

The operations of the TNCs in SEA are organized mostly through their subsidiaries. Transaction costs are important here for the understanding they provide of the organization of economic institutions in LICs. Such coordination costs of the economic system tend to be high in these countries. This leads to a preference for governance forms close to the hierarchical pole on the scale of markets and hierarchies. The local subsidiaries are backed and influenced by a very large organization outside the country in which a given subsidiary is located. With this context, a theory of hierarchical multinationalism is developed. It uses transaction costs to explain the existence of large corporations and is based on three main elements: internalization theory, the eclectic paradigm and the governance-form approach. Of these, the governance-form approach is seen as the most closely applicable, since it takes account of the organizational characteristics of the TNCs more closely than the other two. Nevertheless, the other two approaches focus on certain factors which are important to bear in mind.

By considering both transaction costs and institutional aspects of the organization, an integration can be achieved between different organizational theories and theories of the TNC. The specific form of theory created here is one adapted to the particular context of Eastern Asia. In the theory, account is taken both of economic and of non-economic institutions.

The book is based on an empirical study of the operations of 28 subsidiaries of 17 European transnational corporations in SEA during the period 1984 to 1991.

2. The Transnational Corporation as an Economic Institution

Transnational corporations based in Western Europe and North America share particular traits that distinguish them from companies indigenous to Eastern Asia. This makes it possible to identify what tends to be characteristic of a specific Western European approach to business and to compare this with what can be termed the Japanese, the Korean and the Chinese business approach, these constituting the three most dominating business systems in Eastern Asia (Whitley, 1990, 1992). In this book, such business systems are considered as economic institutions. According to Whitley (1992, pp. 225-38), the authority structure of Western European corporations differs from that of Eastern Asian companies as follows:

1. It is less personal, involves specifications of a more formal character, is more restricted in scope, and is more focused to a greater extent on individual activities.
2. There is a much clearer separation of organizational authority and family authority, especially as compared with Chinese family businesses and with the Korean 'Chaebol'.
3. Personal trust is less crucial, particularly when compared with Chinese family businesses. Instead, greater reliance is placed on institutionally-based trust.
4. There is greater emphasis on formal means or procedures of coordination and control.
5. Formal contracts are more important.
6. There is greater formal specification of individual roles, this having largely to do with the greater specification and standardization of jobs across different firms and different industries. Thus, whereas in Europe occupational structure is more horizontal, in Eastern Asia it is more vertical, an occupation being more strongly bound to a particular company. Related to this aspect is that of professionalization, which is more dominant in Europe.

The last three points, in particular, have facilitated the growth of large managerial hierarchies in European TNCs. Another major difference in the respective authority structures concerns the relations between the business in question and the state, which in Europe are more reciprocal, symmetric and short term, whereas in Eastern Asia they are more state-dominated, unbalanced and long term. In most West European countries except the UK, firms traditionally operate within credit-based financial systems. In the US businesses are more capital-market based. In Korea financial systems are controlled by the state, whereas in Japan they are mostly internalized within the specific company system (the 'Keiretsu'). In Chinese firms they are often internalized within the family-based system. In Eastern Asia financial systems are thus less market-based.

Whitley (1992) has analysed the institutional background of the major characteristics of the economic institution of main concern here, namely the European corporation. Compared with East Asian firms and the business systems they represent, European firms are considerably less influenced by pre-industrial institutions, the historical continuity in Europe being much less. Some of the major non-economic institutional characteristics of European as compared with Eastern Asian countries are the following:

1. There are more autonomous formal legal systems, providing a much higher degree of legal formalization and of rule-bound authority.
2. Institutional mechanisms for establishing trust are more fully developed.
3. The individual is more clearly separated from the family as the basic social unit.
4. Greater importance is attached to horizontal and secondary groupings, for example regarding occupations and skills.
5. The common heritage of Christianity is present; it is insignificant in Eastern Asia.
6. A liberal democratic political system exists, it is not found much in Eastern Asia, where the political system is much more strongly influenced by pre-historical institutions that go back several thousand years, for example Confucian ethics (Pye, 1985).
7. The labour movement is stronger.

Such differences in institutional characteristics between Europe and Eastern Asia are accompanied by corresponding differences in the educational and training systems.

THE WESTERN EUROPEAN CORPORATION

Although institutional pluralism regarding non-economic institutions is in fact greater in Europe than in Eastern Asia, the focus of the book is on traits common to Western European TNCs, and how these traits differ from those of Eastern Asian firms and social systems. The traits of Western European TNCs, as alluded to above, are in basic accordance with the general institutional traits that were taken up in Chapter 1, namely the Judeo-Christian and Greco-Hellenistic traditions of order, symmetry, linearity, and individuality. To these can be added such characteristics as rationality or calculation and a strong dependence on unknown others, signified by calculative behaviour and the importance placed on common values. These basic institutional factors exist in various forms. European TNCs, for example, have been strongly influenced in recent times by North American management philosophies which call for a decentralized organizational structure and treat accountability as being essential. The resulting structure embodies the common traits of individuality, linearity, symmetry, order and rationality.

Modern institutional economic theory that deals with large corporations is used to further specify the Western European corporation as an economic institution, specifically the new-institutional economic theory developed by Williamson (1975, 1979, 1981, 1985). A consideration of the fundamental assumptions of this theory shows it to be largely based on the institutional characteristics discussed above. Order, for example, is represented in the theory by governance forms, and rationality by efficiency. As with economic theories in general, this theory takes the individual as its starting point. According to this theory, hierarchies are more efficient than markets in effectuating transactions, when they place more effective check on opportunism in combination with small-numbers exchange relationships through a more formalized authority structure, and through information impactedness being less due to the information and control systems that a hierarchy possess (Jansson, 1993). This allows conflicts to more efficiently be solved within the organization. Organizations, generally, are also superior to individuals in the compilation and processing of complex information due to the sequential processes involved. Internal organization, or unified governance,[1] engenders both trust and co-operation, which limits opportunistic influences. If opportunism, information impactedness and uncertainty prevail, however, then the disadvantages normally associated with the market may become evident within an organization. This can increase internal transaction costs and make it more rational under such circumstances to shift transactions to the market, provided there is a functioning market in which there are other companies prepared to conduct transactions at a lower cost.

The idea of linearity can be seen in the sequential processes referred to above. The idea of symmetry is also discernible in the trade-offs involved, as well as in the relationship of various governance forms to each other. The institutional mechanisms for establishing trust are a critical element in governance-forms theory, in terms of which institutionally-based trust is more important than individual trust. The various factors involved in the authority structure of Western European corporations are represented within governance-forms theory. Formal contracts and formal means of coordination and control are essential ingredients of the theory, which also foresees a high degree of formal specification of individual roles. The theory is very much reflective of the more autonomous legal systems in the West, which in North America, where the theory originated, may be even more pronounced. There is thus a high degree of legal formalization of the various governance forms generally and a basic authority of rules in the internal governance form (unified governance). Since such characteristics of the theory were found in the present context to be too dominant, they needed to be modified somewhat.

Various external and internal governance forms provide a framework or a set of broad categories for the organizing of transactions. Although this book primarily takes up internal transactions, it is important to consider the relation of these to external transactions. This is done mainly in Chapter 4, where the characteristics of the three main types of external economic institutions, namely market governance, bilateral governance and trilateral governance, are discussed.

THE TRANSNATIONAL M-FORM

TNCs' operations in developing countries are usually carried on by subsidiaries. A transaction-cost model assumes TNCs to operate in developing countries through subsidiaries they control rather than directly through the markets. This organizational aspect is one discussed by Hennart (1982). According to the latter, there are three main cases, in which interdependences between the units of a TNC system are poorly organized by the markets. The first case is characterized by recurrent transactions of intermediate products that have few alternative uses or substitutes and that are characterized by large transaction-specific investments. The second case concerns recurrent transactions of non-patentable know-how and/or goodwill. The third case is one in which the distribution of the parent company's products requires the joint efforts of the manufacturer and the distributor, and in which control by contractual means is costly. All three of these general cases are relevant to the specific cases studied in this book. Hennart summarizes:

> We would expect sales and extractive subsidiaries to be wholly owned, and innovating firms to show a marked preference for wholly owned subsidiaries, especially if they are committed to the continuous improvement of products and processes. On the other hand, multinationals will be more prone to joint-venture subsidiaries that produce different products than the parent, that rely on different trade names, that are mainly oriented to local markets, and that are not involved in the exchange of knowledge with other units of the firm. (Ibid. p. 152)

In this connection, it is important to note, however, that the issue of how economic institutions are organized is also affected by non-economic institutions. Governments, for example, can regulate internalization by instituting ownership rules for foreign subsidiaries. This is discussed further at the end of this chapter.

TNCs often prefer to operate in developing countries through controlled subsidiaries, or on the basis of similar arrangements involving, for example, the ownership of production units. It is usually important that the TNC control to some extent the vertical product structure of the subsidiary, particularly those parts of it relating to the non-patentable core of the firm.

A TNC aggregates an incredible number and amount of differing transactions. Why are all of them internalized within a single hierarchy? Also, how is the total set of transactions related to the much smaller set of transactions that take place in a specific market? The answer to the first question is to be found in the transaction advantages or the advantages of common governance this involves (Dunning, 1988a). A TNC has built up a capability, expressed in its multinational organization, for internalizing transactions in various markets. This organization very much influences whether or not transactions are internalized in a specific geographical area such as SEA. This provides at least a partial answer to the second question that was raised. How the TNC's capabilities relating to common governance are utilized in SEA depends on the specific advantages of, or incentives for, internalization within that region, together with the locational advantages and other type of ownership advantages for the firm this provides, advantages which represent asset advantages. The transnational M-form is the main type of unified governance form taken up here.[2] The main characteristics of this form of economic institution are developed below.

To deal in an adequate way with the internal organization of transactions, it is necessary to take account of the internal organization costs of a TNC, which are handled in only a rudimentary way by internalization theory. Even when these costs are incorporated directly into the theory, as Hennart (1982) and Dunning (1988a) have done, the result does not necessarily become a theory of hierarchical multinationalism. Rather, it became an economic theory focused in Hennart's (1982) case on property rights and measurement costs, and in Dunning's (1988a,b) case on ownership-specific and internalization-incentive advantages. In this book these and other organizational aspects are dealt with in a manner based partly on Williamson's governance-form theory. This allows transactions to be dimensionalized and to be related to different governance forms.

Also, the views of Calvet (1980), and to some extent those of Teece (1986), serve as a basis here for developing an organizational theory pertaining to international and multinational organizations, one which stresses the advantages of the internal efficiency found in such organizations and places special emphasis on the concept of organization costs.

Calvet (1980) describes a TNC as being a multi-product, multi-factory, multi-level, multi-hierarchical and multinational organization. Just as internal organization does in general, the M-form reduces transaction costs through utilization both of internal cross-border markets and of the assets it has available within foreign markets (the transaction cost factor). The M-form of TNC also possesses the overall company-specific assets which are needed (the strategic cost factor).[3] In addition, it also takes advantage of country-specific localization factors in its international operations, e.g. in production (the location factor). As with all firms engaged in international operations, a firm of this sort is also faced with such transactional disadvantages compared with local firms as experiencing greater uncertainty regarding the local market, due for example to political, cultural and social factors.

However, the M-form type of organization involves more than just this, its likewise possessing a divisionalized organizational structure with a high capability for internal control and strategic decision-making. For a multi-dimensional corporation, a multi-divisional type of organization (the M-form) is usually more efficient than a functional type (the U-form). Through a segmentation of various units and a separation of strategic and operative decisions, the M-form suffers less than the U-form from bounded rationality and counteracts sub-optimization more effectively through measures aimed at the avoidance of opportunistic behaviour. In addition, the M-form has quite a different incentive structure. Its efficiency is derived from three main factors: decisions (the informational or cognitive aspect), control and incentives. These three factors and the corresponding aspects of the theory will be dealt with at some depth in the book by analysing the characteristics of the multinational firm seen as an M-form of organization, the different controls of organizational behaviour which are present being emphasized.

Separate units of such an organization can be organized either as divisions or as legal entities in the form of product companies and market companies owned by the parent company. The term M-form is normally restricted to the former type of organization, whereas the latter type is referred to as the H-form (holding company). The main difference concerns how strategic decision-making and internal controls are organized. The parent company in the H-form, a holding company, has a low capacity for both these aspects. Its main task is to run the internal capital market by allocating investment capital (finance) among the various companies of the group. It often pools resources, aggregating dividends and putting together financial reports.

Although most of the TNCs studied in this project are organized as a group of companies, they can be classified as M-form organizations. The reason for this is that the strategic decision-making and internal controls carried out by the parent company cover a much broader spectrum of activities than financial matters alone. The responsibility for the different companies within the group is usually divided among various directors, termed the executive general management (EGM) or group management (GM).

The transnational M-form can readily be equated with the three main strategic principles identified by Bartlett and Ghoshal (1989) for how different TNCs are organized. These authors found there to be three main types of organization forms – global organizational, multinational organizational, and international organizational – and three major principles corresponding to these – the principles of global efficiency, national responsiveness, and technological development and transfer (organizational learning). All three principles can be seen as relevant to the present and future organization of a TNC. At the same time, the TNCs that were studied in the project differ in the way these principles are organized and combined. Global efficiency, which is achieved through economies of scale and through scope, and is closely related to the standardization of markets and of products, is considered here within the context of global integration, the efficiency concept being reserved for use in connection with the overall organizational principle characterizing the TNC as a whole. The three strategic principles of global integration, national responsiveness and organizational learning are all subsumed under this overall principle. Since in the transnational M-form, efficiency is achieved by reducing transaction costs, a specification of these costs must consider all three principles, a matter taken up below.

Strategic Advantages

The strategies employed by an organization of the transnational M-form type can be interpreted from an institutional perspective. This means the competition on world markets being viewed as 'a struggle between different ways of structuring forms of economic organization and the dominant social institutions which generated and reproduced them' (Whitley, 1992, p. 250). This implies, as already indicated, there is no overriding and general efficiency concept valid for all business systems, one which any firm would endeavour to achieve and in accordance with which markets should function generally. Rather, as stressed in this book, Western European TNCs appear to operate according to a line of reasoning that differs from that followed by large Japanese companies, which in turn deviates from that followed by Korean or Chinese businesses. Thus, competition within international markets can be said to take place between different forms of economic organization which are institutionally based. The competitive element in the economic organization and the strategic behaviour of Western European TNCs is considered in this section in terms combining Porter's conception of industrial organizational competition with Chamberlain's views on competition (Barney and Ouchi, 1986, pp. 372-80). The competitive behaviour of Western European TNCs is assumed to be based on the exploitation of external market factors and of the firm's unique internal skills, its resources and its distinctive competencies. One major aspect of monopolistic competition is that the firm's being heterogeneous because of its having unique assets with which it can compete. Since both the external market structure and the internal organizational structure of a TNC are intimately related, the company's strategy is closely linked with its organizational characteristics.

This is a basic assumption in theories regarding TNCs, expressed in the eclectic paradigm, for example, as the advantages of ownership. Advantages of this sort, taken up in this section, can be divided into asset advantages and transaction advantages (Dunning, 1988a,b). Asset advantages reflect the unique assets of the firm, those on which monopolistic competition is based. A strength of the eclectic paradigm is that it combines the two main types of competition just referred to and provides a theory regarding how a TNC is affected by its unique assets. Ownership advantages of the asset type can result from structural market imperfections. Dunning (1988b, p. 2) indicates that asset advantages

> arise from the proprietary ownership of specific assets by MNEs vis-à-vis those possessed by other enterprises ... which can only occur in a situation of structural market distortions. (For example, as identified by Bain (1956) as monopoly power, product differentiation, absolute cost barriers and government intervention.)

Such advantages come about through the economics of the integration within the firm of separate value-added activities. A particular strength of the eclectic paradigm, of considerable importance in this context, is the distinction it makes between two types of ownership advantages: asset advantages and transaction advantages. The latter advantage can be defined as

> the capacity of MNE hierarchies vis-à-vis external markets to capture the transactional benefits (or lessen the transactional costs) arising from the common governance of a network of these assets, located in different countries. (*Ibid.*)

A TNC has built up the capacity, through its multinational organization, to internalize transactions in markets, making it possible for it to decide whether, in a specific geographical area such as SEA, transactions should be internalized or not. The readiness of a TNC to do this and thus expand its activities in a new market depends on how conducive the specific circumstances in the region are to transactions. These can be termed the internalization-incentive advantages. They embrace

> the gains arising from co-ordinating the use of complementary assets as well as the benefits replacing the markets for the first kind of advantage (asset advantages) relative, for example, to the licensing of the right of their use within the independent foreign firms. (Dunning, 1988a, p. 123)

Transaction cost can thus be divided up into one factor internal to the TNC, that of the transaction advantages or the advantages of common governance, and one factor external to the TNC, the internalization-incentive advantages. These two major elements in the eclectic paradigm are an important basis for the study. With the introduction into this paradigm of advantages related to transaction costs, the TNC enters the model in its own right. Although, certain general internal characteristics of the firm are expressed as asset advantages, it is first when questions of transaction cost are taken into account that the organizational issue as a whole is introduced into the theory. In the present book on organizational aspects of industrial TNCs, this part of the theory becomes a 'natural' focus. However, because of the only very general character of the eclectic paradigm, it is no more than a point of departure. Indeed, the book penetrates more deeply into the problems of TNCs than this, the theoretical framework of the study being more specific and differentiated than the eclectic paradigm alone, more specific factors being considered.

Strategies of Western European TNCs located in SEA or in other parts of the world are affected both by the asset advantages of being a TNC, and also by the structural market imperfections and locational advantages of a specific area. More important still, such strategies are influenced by the transaction-cost based internalization-incentive advantages of a given region such as Southeast Asia, with the accompanying possibilities of reducing the costs of information, bargaining and enforcement. These costs may be incurred in such ways as in enforcing property rights, in reducing buyer uncertainty, in protecting the quality of the product, in controlling supplies and the conditions of sales, and in controlling market outlets. Internalization-incentive advantages are chiefly transaction-cost based and are the focus of the model, since they determine how the customer/supplier interface is organized. Internal advantages cast further light on the vertical competitive strategies a TNC develops (Jansson, 1993). The conceptions here regarding transaction advantages that may be present for a TNC are developed further in this book based on Williamson's (1985) theory of governance forms. However, as Casson (1987, p. 42) has pointed out:

Williamson's theory, on the other hand, provides a model for how managers make decisions, but lacks the model that describes the environment in which the decisions must be made.

Casson proposes that Williamson's theory should be combined with neoclassical theory regarding location, as well as with internalization theory, so as to compensate for this deficiency. However, this is too narrow an approach for the perspective taken in the present book on Western European TNCs, since it is adequate to too few aspects of the strategic behaviour of these firms, at the same time as the institutional perspective would thus be missed. Regarding the strategic aspect, it is as important to include asset advantages of the firm as it is the structural market imperfections of the local markets. Regarding the latter, describing the environment is insufficient. In studying the decisions and strategies of TNCs in Asia, the applicability there of models that were developed in industrialized countries cannot be taken for granted. The broader institutional environment of such countries also needs to be taken into account (see below).

The traditional competitive advantages of a firm can thus be expressed as asset advantages. Transaction advantages, or the firm's way of organizing internally, represent still another advantage a firm may have. This has far-reaching consequences for how strategy is viewed and studied. The focus is no longer solely on structural market imperfections, as it is in Porter (1980, 1981, 1986), for example.

Three Sets of Interests

Three main goals or rationalities are found within the transnational M-form, one of these being of local and the other two of global concern. Organizational learning is a critical principle for all three of these concerns or sets of interests. The management of the individual market company must respond to local demands and opportunities. Such managers possess strong national interests and function as spokesmen for this rationality of national responsiveness within the TNC. The global product interests, or the principle of global integration, is represented by the management of the product divisions, the product companies, the different business areas, or whatever they may be called within the individual TNCs. Such units have a worldwide responsibility for their products. The task of the executive general management (EGM) at group headquarters is to look after the interests of the group as a whole, e.g. by working as a controller, a coordinator or a mediator. These roles can be performed in such ways as solving conflicts between local or geographic interests and global product interests within a matrix organization. Besides competition for the internal resources of the TNC between these three separate interests, there is also competition among the various product interests and local interests.

Bartlett and Ghoshal (1991) have developed three main types of management roles found within the transnational corporation, which largely correspond with the three sets of interests mentioned above. The strategic role of integrating activities worldwide is delegated to the divisional level by group management and is divided up among several divisions, which in this study are product-based in most cases, but which is also based on the geographic dimension in a few cases. The main function to be performed here is maintenance of global efficiency and competitiveness, for example scale economies, synergies, and competitive advantages on a worldwide scale, by transnational integration of activities. Bartlett and Ghoshal identify three main strategic roles for product division management, namely:

1. a global business strategist;
2. an architect of asset configuration, being responsible for the coordination of key assets and locating them in a manner that supports the strategic objectives;
3. a transnational coordinator, for example in implementing marketing strategy.

For the manager of a subsidiary in a given country there are also three main roles, namely:

1. A bicultural interpreter. The main task here is to integrate local company perspective with group perspective.
2. A defender and representative of the country in question.
3. A front-line implementer of group strategies and policies.

The overall corporate interests are:

1. to create a diverse set of business, functional, and geographic management groups, assigning them specific roles and responsibilities, and presenting in an adequate way the strategic focus and vision;
2. to give each unit organizational legitimacy;
3. to balance and to integrate.

Internal Transaction Costs

The major principle of organizational behaviour within the context of the transnational M-form is efficiency, the reduction in transaction costs serving as a theoretical construct to denote the intention inherent in this principle. Such costs can also be termed inefficiency costs, since the more inefficient an organization is, the higher the transaction costs become. By reducing these costs, organizational efficiency is increased and profits are improved. Three major characteristics of organizational behaviour are frequently mentioned in the organizational literature regarding TNCs or general organization theory, namely decisions, action, and conflicts. These are directly related to efficiency by linking one of these three features to one main type of transaction cost, which is illustrated in Figure 2.1. Thus, the aim of an efficient organization should be to reduce the transaction costs connected not only with decision making, but also with the implementation of decisions and the reduction of the major goal conflicts between different parts of the organization. Three different types of transaction costs can be distinguished, those of information, bargaining and enforcement.

Figure 2.1 Three main aspects of organizational behaviour and their respective transaction costs

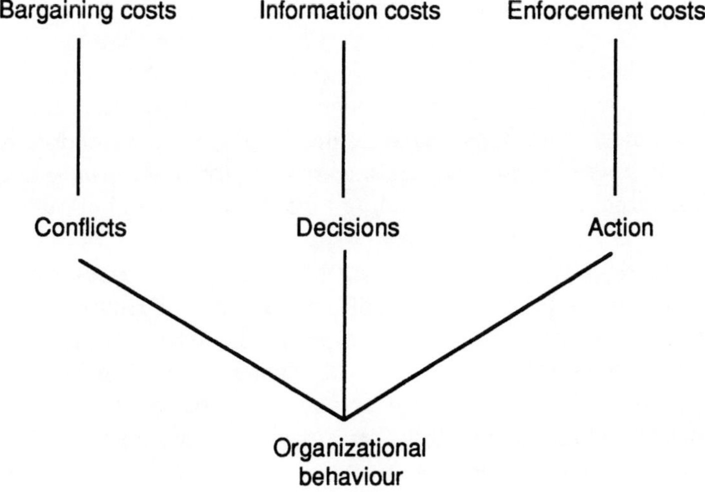

Information costs are connected primarily with decision making, but also with the implementation of decisions and with conflicts. For instance, the worse the decisions which are taken are, the higher the information or transaction costs are and the lower the efficiency is. The costs of finding and compiling the information for a decision (market-specific knowledge) is an example. Such costs particularly concern market information, accounting, and other information systems that influence how strategic planning and budgeting are organized.

Decision making is cognitive in nature and is restricted by bounded rationality. Antagonists are often involved in decision making and conflicts may arise due to opportunistic behaviour. Such behaviour may partly be dishonest, involving, for example, lying or the deliberate distortion of information, but can also include honest disagreements inasmuch as people perceive reality differently (Alchian and Woodward, 1988). Goal conflicts are frequently reinforced by conflicts between honest employees within an organization, who fail to agree. Opportunistic behaviour is partly a consequence of bounded rationality, and partly of self-interests. Employees hired to follow directions, but acting in their own self-interest instead, through on-the-job consumption, for example, can cause considerable loss to a firm and represent a moral hazard.

Conflicts are regarded as a symptom of opportunistic behaviour, and originate mainly in the clashing of the three main goals or rationalities that are found within a TNC.

A critical question in the transnational M-form then is the promoting of both local and global effectiveness in decision making, or making the right trade-off between global integration and local responsiveness. The costs that arise due to the relative freedom given to various interests in a decentralized transnational M-form and to the ensuing bargaining necessary to align these interests and allow definitive action are termed bargaining costs.

However, efficient decisions do not follow automatically from decision makers having the 'right' information. To avoid suboptimization, it is not enough to have an efficient bargaining process. Costs can arise through not acting in accordance with decisions and agreements made regarding transactions in various parts of the TNC. Such problems in implementing decisions are denoted as enforcement costs. Opportunism influences this type of cost as well.

ORGANIZATIONAL CONTROLS

Transaction costs and thus efficiency are in turn influenced by different organizational controls, for instance the organization structure and different information controls. In line with Hechter (1987, pp. 50-1), a distinction can be made between a control capacity, which involves a sanctioning, and monitoring capacity.

> The relationship between control and compliance is intricate for two reasons. In the first place, the group must have sufficient resources at its disposal to effectively reward or punish its members contingent on their level of contribution or performance. This ability to provide what are essentially selective incentives can be called the group's sanctioning capacity. ... The second reason for the intricacy of the relationship between control and compliance is that the group must be able to detect whether individuals comply with their obligations or not. This is its monitoring capacity. Monitoring is problematic because individual behaviour is often difficult to observe, much less to measure. ... Altogether, then, noncompliance with obligations (and with rules of any sort) can have at least two separate roots: it can be due to inadequate sanctioning or to impaired monitoring. Since each of these activities is costly, the total costs of control constitute a severe constraint on any group's ability to attain compliance.

Various organizational controls are utilized in the transnational M-form, these affecting transaction costs differently. There is a trade-off, for instance, between investments in a sanctioning capacity and in a monitoring capacity. Investments in individual self-control and in indirect controls related to the sanctioning capacity reduce the need for investment in the controls that relate to monitoring capacities, particularly of the traditional kind such as behavioural control. Monitoring capacity is largely limited then to performance control and to such input control as socialization. These controls are analysed in greater detail below.

To summarize, the theoretical organization costs of the transnational M-form are costs for getting information regarding decisions concerning transactions. Bargaining costs are costs for resolving conflicts between different interests regarding decision making and the implementation of decisions. Enforcement costs, lastly, are costs related to taking appropriate actions. There are many potential combinations for connecting these main types of transaction costs with one another through finding the best combination of controls. For instance, a tighter control of conflict resolution in order to improve the implementation of decisions may reduce bargaining and enforcement costs through improvement in the implementation of decisions. Such increased control may also result in spin-offs regarding information costs, complicating the trade-offs even more. Conflicts may generate information concerning both decision making and the implementation of decisions, the gains achieved being passed on to other parts of the organization, improving decision making generally. This tighter control may be less efficient than one might expect, since reducing conflicts may decrease spin-off effects on information costs, these latter costs increasing.

A distinction can be made, therefore, between the costs for decision making, for conflict resolution and for enforcement, all three of which can be designated as control costs. Efficiency in the organization can be achieved by reducing these costs, something which can be done through organizational controls. Such control costs are the hierarchical equivalent of transaction costs and thus correspond to the bureaucratic costs referred to by Coase (1937) and by Williamson (1985). These latter costs, or internal transaction costs, tend to increase with the size of the firm. The control costs for decisions, actions, and conflicts are the main organization costs of the transnational M-form, which can therefore be viewed as a control structure. Such costs are affected by the design of the formal organization, by how the responsibility for various decisions is assigned, and by the creation of specific positions such as those of integrators with the task of reducing conflicts. Temporary solutions to this end can be achieved through teams, coordinating committees, task forces, and the like. Alignments can also be accomplished through some kind of 'contract', for example the budget system.

Each of the three types of transaction costs include both costs for establishing contracts and ex-post costs for administering, informing about, monitoring, and enforcing the performance that is promised contractually (Williamson, 1975). Measurement costs are all-pervading, being present under conditions of all three types: of bargaining, of decision making about transactions, and of enforcing decisions. These costs are to a considerable degree a function of the complexity of the situation, that is of how easy it is to measure the factors of interest. These transaction costs are in turn determined by three additional factors: uncertainty, bounded rationality and opportunism. These latter factors vary with the environment, depending, for example, on whether an industrial structure, cultural or legal structure, or government policies are involved.

Fundamental Controls

Within the transnational M-form there is a rich repertoire of organizational controls that influence transaction costs. Three fundamental types of control are derived from this transaction-cost approach to internal organization: ownership control, market control, and hierarchical control. Ownership control through shareholding and an own representation on the board is a basic strategic control which may be used, for example, to decentralize the organizational structure by giving divisions or subsidiaries a more independent standing. Research has shown that TNCs usually prefer to control their operations by majority ownership. There are restrictions on this, however, in certain Southeast Asian countries, for example in Malaysia and Indonesia. Market control is the second type of fundamental control, one that is particularly strong if a unit is incorporated. A separate and incorporated firm operates more independently in the product market and is therefore controlled to a greater degree by the market. Such external control reduces the need for internal control. As will be shown, market control by the group is stronger in small market companies in countries far from Europe than in large market companies in the major markets. The incorporation of its units provides various advantages to a given group. The group's flexibility is enhanced through this making it easier for the group to buy and sell units. Finances are also improved by the group's being able to sell shares in its daughter companies. Taxes can be reduced by adapting the legal status of subsidiaries to the laws of the respective countries, or by utilizing the possibilities created by the incorporation of units for manipulating transfer prices. Transfer prices may also be used to circumvent government rules, for example exchange regulations. Legal status is thus a key to possibilities for varying the financial control of a TNC. As will be discussed later, such financial controls are opposed to the use of other forms of internal control, for example a performance-oriented transfer-pricing system. Hierarchical control, the third basic form of control, is mainly executed through such internal measures as those related to the spatial organization structure, or through the use of information control as exemplified by rules, or through output control in the form of transfer prices.

These three fundamental types of control lie at the basis of the more specific types of control referred to here – organization structure, information control and behaviour control, output control, and input control – all of which are taken up in Figure 2.2.

Figure 2.2 Internal controls

Spatial Organization Structure

- Departmentalization in the grouping of organizational units and shaping the formal structure.
- Centralization or decentralization of decision making, depending upon the hierarchy of formal authority.
- Ownership pattern.

Information Controls

Rules
Information stored in texts (formalization and standardization): written policies, rules, job descriptions, and standard procedures, and instruments such as manuals, charts, etc., often used in the planning and budget system.

Prices
Transfer prices stored as numbers.

Praxis
Stored knowledge transferred through

- *lateral or cross-departmental/divisional/company relations*: direct managerial contact, temporary or permanent teams, task forces, committees, managers with integration tasks, and integration departments.
- *informal communication*: personal contacts among managers, management trips, meetings, conferences, transfer of managers.

Behaviour Control

Orders, advice, dialogue.

Output (Performance) Control

Financial performance, technical reports, sales and marketing data, largely organized through a planning and budget system.

Input Control

Socialization, building an organizational culture of known and shared strategic objectives and values through training, career path management, measurement and reward systems, informal communication (see above), and the transfer of managers.

Sources: This information is largely based on Collin (1990), Larsson (1989), Martinez and Jarillo (1989, 1991), and Gupta and Govindarajan (1991).

The Spatial Organization Structure

The organizational structure provides the setting in which decision making, decision implementation and conflict resolution take place. One major question addressed here and already raised in Chapter 1 is why the physical (geographic) and psychic distance between international operations, or in short the spatial dimension, is internalized within a single transnational hierarchy rather than being externalized through the markets of various countries by use of agents or other intermediaries. This spatial dimension of an organization, of primary importance in international operations, leads to the structure of organizations in which it plays a leading role being classified as being of the 'spatial M-form'.

Williamson (1981, p. 1550) speaks in this connection of a hierarchical decomposition principle of internal organization.

> Internal organization should be designed in such a way as to effect quasi-independence between the parts, the high frequency dynamics (operating activities) and low frequency dynamics (strategic planning) should be clearly distinguished, and incentives should be aligned within and between components so as to promote both local and global effectiveness.

The basic principle with which Williamson is concerned here involves information and cognitive aspects of organizational decision-making, including bounded rationality, as well as behavioural aspects, in particular opportunism.

In transnational terms, this means creating an efficient vertical division of the organization into semi-autonomous geographic units in order to balance incentives and controls. The degree of autonomy varies between different units. Those in far-off and culturally distant markets tend to be the most autonomous. Such an arrangement is efficient as long as it does not conflict with the global interests of the group or lead to sub-optimization. Large parts of such subsidiaries, mainly those parts at a lower hierarchical level, can be separated so as to function on their own in such matters as transactions both with local customers and suppliers and with government authorities. The parts of subsidiaries involving the work of the lower-level staff and of blue-collar workers, which differ a lot from one country to another, can also be largely run at the local level. The overall control of subsidiaries, on the other hand, cannot be held separate from the functioning of transnational organization as a whole and must thus be integrated into the work of the group. This makes the control strategy towards management very important in the 'spatial M-form'. This is a matter considered in greater detail below. The degree of vertical decomposition can be hypothesized to be greater internationally than domestically in the M-form, since it could be inefficient to superimpose a global control strategy on a local one, where local incentive systems, for example, could be destroyed by an uncritical implementation of too large a part of the global incentive system at the local level, something which could make transaction costs rise sky-high. This is a classical issue within the area of human resource management of multinational enterprises (see, for example, Robock and Simmonds, 1989; Bartlett and Ghoshal, 1989).

Regional organization

The vertical division of a transnational organization into semi-autonomous geographic units can be carried out in two steps: at the regional and at the local level. Doing so at the regional level, where global and local interests are both in focus, is efficient if the transaction costs are lower for the locating of functions at the regional than at the global or the local level. Examples of the relative costs involved are given by Grosse (1982, p. 116):

> (1) reducing travel time of executives who frequently visit affiliates to monitor their operations and potentially to develop regional strategies;
> (2) placing the managers of the regional headquarters in a location with excellent communications, both to the home office and to affiliates;
> (3) centralizing information at a manageable (i.e. regional) level, rather than overwhelming the home office with it, and rather than allowing excessive autonomy to each affiliate by not centralizing information at all (agglomeration economy (a));
> (4) gaining access to a pool of talented potential managers and staff, who are familiar with the language and culture of the region (agglomeration economy (b)).

The main purpose of a regional organization is to manage, control and coordinate regional activities. The more differentiated business in the various countries is, in terms of the industries represented and legislative and cultural matters, for example, the greater the need is for business being integrated, even if only loosely. Regional integration allows for greater responsiveness to local conditions than global integration does and for the degree of transactions between the local market companies and group management being reduced. If the distance between a given region and headquarters is large, a representative of group management may be relocated to the region to increase efficiency through a reduction in information and enforcement costs.

Parochial interests are better controlled through a regional organization, which can also reduce bargaining costs within the group. In addition, through staff being moved there, management can still be further improved.

Information Controls

Control through information that is provided is crucial within the transnational M-form, since individuals need information about suitable and unsuitable actions for making decisions and in order to be able to act in a coordinated way towards given ends. Within the governance structure at hand, organizational behaviour is controlled through three main carriers of information: price, rules, and praxis (Larsson, 1989, chapter 5).[4] Price, which is quantified in character, is the main carrier of information within markets, it being the primary factor controlling and coordinating individual actions. Rules are formal in nature and express verbally in text basic standards of behaviour. Praxis, in contrast, is stored or amassed knowledge providing informal guidance concerning how to act. It consists of implicit rules based on knowledge, for example of how a particular governance form or organization functions, a large part of that knowledge being tacit; in addition, it includes activities that carry established or learned know-how. The control provided by these three information carriers is closely linked with habits, which can be defined as routinized behaviour, customs being a highly similar concept. Information controls result in certain habitual behaviour, habits of various sorts being transmitted to individuals through prices, rules and praxis. According to J. Kornai:

> stabilized and routinized behaviour establishes and reproduces a set of rules and norms 'fixed by habit, convention, tacit or legally supported acceptance or conformity'. (Quoted by Hodgson, 1988, p. 132)

Price control, as already indicated, is a critical mode of information control, one related mainly to performance control but also partly representing input control. Price control is executed through an organizational-internal transfer price system often administered by special units. Various models of the market, ranging from that of a perfect market (involving theoretical shadow prices) to some kind of bilateral governance form, can be utilized as a basis for the internal pricing system. The savings in transaction costs vary with how the transfer price system is organized, becoming greater the more closely a neoclassical perfect market model is approached. This latter model cannot be employed, however, since the transfer pricing system is incomplete due to its asset-specificities. Such a less than transparent managed price system requires periodic revisions, which opens up the possibility of various organizational units manipulating prices to their own advantage. Prices can also be determined by bargaining between different units, a matter which affects transaction costs. A high-powered incentive system such as this also has potential side-effects, for example that of short-sighted behaviour, which can lead to the over-utilization of assets and to suboptimization, which reduce the long-term efficiency of the group. Internal pricing may therefore be replaced or supplemented by lower-powered incentives such as salary increases and promotion systems combined with periodic monitoring of individual performance, or of the performance of the respective units. The importance of price controls varies with such factors as the legal status of the separate units within the group and the types of connection between them (e.g. transaction-specific investments), matters analysed more fully in Chapters 4 and 6. Some of the drawbacks of price controls may be overcome by socialization. Thus, these two major types of control can complement and support each other.

Behaviour Control

Within the framework which organizational structure and information controls provide, behaviour control or process control may be used for controlling decision making, the implementation of decisions, and the resolution of conflict. Part of this control is direct, in the form of personal surveillance and the like, involving orders, advice or dialogue, for example. Part of it too is indirect. The organizational structure, for example, can be viewed as a control infrastructure, which exerts an indirect control over behaviour through the formal structure it possesses and the hierarchy of formal authority it contains. Indirect behaviour control also takes place through rules, which were just shown to also represent a form of information control. Rules are often established through the formalization and standardization of existing information, for example through preparing statements of policy, job descriptions, manuals or charts.

Output Control

Both the traditional direct bureaucratic control of subordinates and the indirect control of them through rules, procedures, manuals and the like tend to be of limited efficiency in organizations of the highly decentralized multi-level, multi-hierarchical and multinational M-form type. There, the planning and budgetary systems, which aim at controlling the results of organizational behaviour, or the output, represent more usual means of control. Creating an internal price system provides a basic foundation for such control. The information control means of price also represents a major information carrier in output or performance control, its tending to be created within the framework of a planning and budgetary system that provides objectives and performance standards for individual action. Marketing, purchasing, production and financial performance are all controlled through a reporting system and an internal price system.

Input Control

Another important means for the indirect control of behaviour involves methods employed to select those persons who are to belong to the organization and to socialize them as regards the corporate values and beliefs. This represents input control. Both the socialization aspect of such input control and the performance control achieved through the setting of internal prices are given special emphasis in this book. In the transnational M-form, these two types of control are more critical to efficiency than are the more traditional bureaucratic controls that characterize the U-form. Since control in the M-form is mostly of an indirect sort, direct intervention is very selective, top management only intervening when direct control yields net gains in efficiency.[5]

Socialization is thus one basic means of control for the transnational M-form organization, which may endeavour to integrate its autonomous units globally through indoctrinating its managers concerning the values and ways of thinking of the group, there being a transfer of information, influence and persons between the various group units. Through its facilitating such transfers, the budgeting system may also become an important mode of socialization.

Praxis is stored knowledge about how to act in a certain situation, it in turn being controlled by input control, for example by socialization concerned with influencing the values found within the organization.

Input control may be achieved through career path management, through the transfer of managers, through measurement and reward systems, and through informal communication. Informal organizational aspects tend to be highly important here, especially if a transnational solution is sought (Bartlett and Ghoshal, 1989), informal communication occurring, for example through personal contacts among managers, the holding of conferences and the transfer of managers, all of which can influence the know-how of the individuals involved. Informal communication can also come about in connection with lateral or cross-divisional contacts, direct managerial contacts, and the formation of temporary teams. More formal situations such as courses and the like can also be arranged for providing insight into how the organization works and how it should work.

IMPACT OF NON-ECONOMIC INSTITUTIONS

TNCs were analysed above in terms of their representing economic institutions. Usually, the operations of TNCs in developing countries are studied with the implicit assumption that the economic institutions of different countries are so similar that TNCs can operate in basically the same way in Indonesia, for example, as in the USA. To employ the same strategies and establish the same sort of organization in quite different countries reflects such an assumption of the economic institutions being basically similar and being readily transferable between countries. As already indicated, this is an unacceptable premise from an institutional perspective, particularly when the institutional differences involved are as great as they in fact are between industrialized countries and those LICs considered here. The approach of this book is thus institutional, taking account of the specific characteristics of the institutions within which economic actions are embedded. The TNCs involved all originated within the context of the economic institutions of Western-style capitalism. The effectiveness of transplanting the economic institution that such a firm represents to quite a different institutional setting depends on the inherent characteristics of such an institution and the possibilities of matching them to those of the domestic institutions of the developing country. Competition takes place then between such an imported economic institution and other economic institutions, many of them locally based. Differences between the basic institutional frameworks involved are not dealt with in such new-institutional theories as transaction-cost theory.

This is unfortunate, since the effects of a transfer are dependent not only on the efficient working of the governance forms in question but also on the non-economic institutional framework within which these market institutions are embedded, involving for example government, the legal system, the culture, and professional structures. The norms, laws and rules of these institutions closely affect the transaction process.

As indicated earlier, transaction costs vary with uncertainty, bounded rationality and opportunism. Differences in the non-economic institutional framework influence, on the basis of these factors, the economic institutions involved. How the non-economic institutional framework affects transaction costs and then economic institutions is considered in this section. Calvet and Naim (1981), for example, hypothesize that the unified governance form is more common in developing countries than in developed market economies. This hypothesis is based on an analysis of a number of differences between developed and developing countries in the postulates involved, as taken from a more general transaction-cost theory of Williamson's (1975). This is shown in Figure 2.3.

Figure 2.3 Economic institutions and non-economic institutions

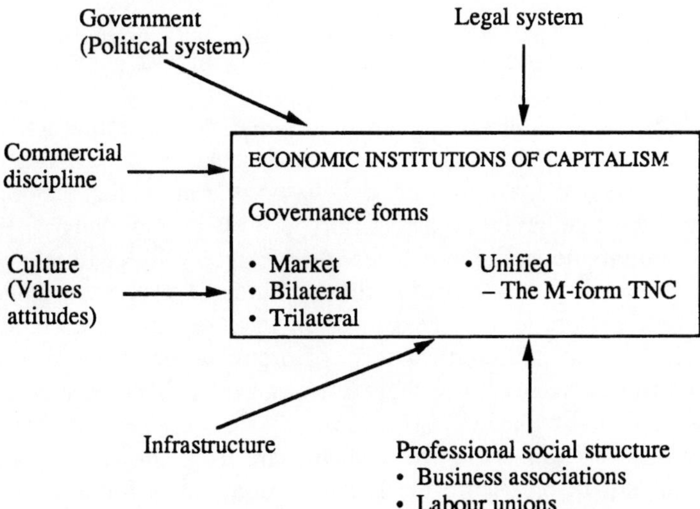

One important difference between the institutional framework of a TNC in its European operations and the institutional framework tending to characterize SEA is the *shortage of qualified management resources* in the latter setting, something which limits the technical capacity available for the processing and analysis of information. The impact on transaction costs both of limited rationality and of conditions of uncertainty and complexity tends here, therefore, to be greater. Such a tendency is also strengthened by the fact that the complexities of the modern economic world are comparatively new to these LICs and that *information is often more imperfect and scarce.* Statistics there are hardly reliable and there is a lack of an efficient infrastructure for generating and utilizing information. As already indicated, government policies are organized in a different way in LICs, few sectors of economic activity there working without direction from or participation by, the government.

Calvet and Naim specify factors which contribute to making the combination of opportunist conduct and occurrence of situations involving economic relations among small numbers of participants more frequent in developing countries and which also are relevant for the situation in Southeast Asia. For one thing, the legal system tends to provide insufficient safeguards concerning reciprocity and the faithful compliance with contractual conditions, the legal systems themselves and other institutional factors seeming to have reinforced such traditional business practices of the overseas Chinese as

> secrecy, reliance on personal ties and family members and a preference for flexibility and direct personal control of employees. (Whitley, 1992, p. 197)

The relatively weak legal system, combined with commercial discipline that differs from that in Western Europe, tends to result in a higher propensity for opportunist behaviour among the economic actors in SEA than among those in Europe. This is something particularly common among Chinese firms. An important factor in this context is the weak protection of different kinds of property rights in SEA. These factors just referred to result in European TNCs tending to develop a more hierarchical form of organization in their Southeast Asian operations than in their European ones. This is in accordance with Williamson (1975), where a basic statement is that the development of hierarchies follows in part from the opportunistic behaviour and in part from the situation commonly found of there being only a small number of participants involved. Additional factors that could be mentioned are the predominance of small markets, and of narrow capital markets in particular, together with a lack of specialized human resources.

The conditions in SEA are thus highly conducive to European TNCs employing administrative hierarchies rather than the market for the conduct of economic exchange, and to their controlling their subsidiaries there carefully (Dunning, 1988a).

At the same time, Calvet and Naim discuss the reasons for organizational failures that tend to impede any total substitution of hierarchies for markets in developing countries. They note that there are political restrictions on the size of companies, restrictions which limit the scope of monopolistic advantages. The resulting disadvantages in terms of potential size create particular problems due to the shortage of qualified human resources in SEA and clashes between such institutional factors as culture, which lead, because of a high level of entrepreneurship on the part of many of the more qualified native employees, and difficulties in socializing the native employees in accordance with company aims, to a marked propensity for native employees to leave the company. In short, loss of control over a subsidiary occurs more readily in SEA than in Europe.

Native governmental policies of restricting entry sometimes prevent TNCs from establishing subsidiaries in the region and force them to employ external organizational forms such as distributors and agents.

Culture is another important non-economic institution that influences the local organization of European TNCs in the region and the integration of local business activities with those of the group at large. Culture is in fact one of the most important factors leading to the differentiation of control over the subsidiaries, particularly since the local culture in SEA differs so much from the culture in the main markets. The Chinese-dominated business culture in this region has certain characteristics that appear to justify a different type of control being exercised over subsidiaries than over their European counterparts. Among these characteristics are those of the culture being highly relation- and family-oriented, the Chinese themselves tending to be entrepreneurial, pragmatic, clannish, superstitious, materialistic and oriented to matters of saving face. They can also be said to have a traditional acquiescence to, and desire for, hierarchical authority and a limited capacity to remain united long in a common cause, except within their inner circles. These traits are combined in different ways in business. One example is that of the traditional family-owned network of small firms that resembles the Chinese family system itself. Here, the combined emphasis on family, hierarchy, and face leads to a kind of closed network of business units in which there is tight coupling and a strong hierarchy within the individual unit but a loose and non-hierarchical organization across units.

CONCLUSIONS

The institutional background of European TNCs was dealt with in this chapter, their being characterized as economic institutions driven by transactions. Various characteristics of the transactions determine whether a TNC will be organized internally or externally. The degree of asset-specificity, the frequency of transactions, and the prevalence of differing degrees of opportunism and of bounded rationality, for example, result in various information, bargaining and enforcement costs. The reduction in such costs which can be achieved varies with how decisions are made and implemented in transactions, with how conflicts of interest are solved, and with how decisions, actions and conflicts are controlled. If the costs involved become lower if authority serves as the primary mode, an internalization of decisions, and actions, and of conflict resolution tends to come about. Alternatively, if a bilateral mode or a trilateral mode is less costly, an externalization of these matters is more likely.

The transnational M-form was considered at length. Its efficiency can be seen as due to a high capacity for strategic decision-making and for internal control, together with a particular type of incentive structure. These factors are manifested in the main types of control that apply, namely control by organizational structure, information controls, behaviour control, output control and input control. Efficiency is achieved through a reduction in transaction costs regarding three major aspects of organizational behaviour: decision making, the implementation of decisions, and the resolution of goal conflicts between different parts of the organization. Efficiency of organizational structure is achieved through the hierarchical decomposition principle of internal organization, where a vertical division of the transnational organization into semi-autonomous geographic units is carried out in two main steps: for regions and for countries. Normally this means a high decentralization through a hierarchy of formal authority. The three information controls are rules, prices and praxis, the mix of which varies with the operating conditions. Three other types of control are also used to attain efficiency in the organization, namely behavioural control, output control and input control.

These economic institutions of capitalism tend, at the same time, to be constrained in SEA by various non-economic institutions, the effects of which can be understood in terms of transaction cost. Particular local governmental policies, a weaker legal system and ethical standards in business which differ from those predominant in Europe can readily lead to uncertainty in business and make opportunistic behaviour common. Transaction costs then become high, resulting in a strong tendency for unified governance to be established. Government is an important factor in business in SEA, often taking a direct part in organizing transactions. Public fiat, for example, takes place through a planning system. The state has an indirect effect on economic institutions through the manipulation of other non-economic institutions, for example of the legal system.

NOTES

1. Note the difference between unified governance and the unitary organization form (U-form). Unified governance amounts to the internal organization of transactions, which in turn corresponds to the external organization forms: the market, together with bilateral and trilateral governance. Unitary organization, in contrast, is a functional organization structure, normally compared with the multi-divisional organization structure or the M-form (Williamson, 1975, 1979).
2. Cable (1988, pp. 35-6) concludes the following, after reviewing 14 studies of the economic performance of the M-form:

   The multi-divisional corporation is an important economic institution, not least because of the huge amount of economic activity which goes on under its control. Historical evidence clearly shows that the M-form innovation has allowed giant firms to survive, and to solve the problems attendant upon policies of growth and diversification which might otherwise have led to their downfall. What is less clear is whether it can be said to have resulted in behaviour significantly closer to the neoclassical model than would otherwise have been the case. Though early statistical results of the M-form hypothesis to that effect were interpreted as supporting the hypothesis, subsequent evidence has been mixed. Some of this evidence suggests that there may be differences in the extent of potential M-form gains in different national settings and, more generally, that the benefits may depend on context as well as the intrinsic properties of M-form itself. In short, it can safely be said that, though not all M-form adoptions have been entirely successful, M-form has often been a triumph in business efficiency terms. But its effects in broader, economic efficiency terms (which are *a priori* ambiguous for welfare) have yet to be established beyond reasonable doubt.
3. The importance for a theory of the TNC of this strategic factor or ownership advantage as it is called in terms of the eclectic paradigm, is debatable. Casson (1987, p. 34), believes that this factor can be excluded from the theory:

   Internalization liberates the theory of the MNE from dependence on the postulates of the Hymer-Kindleberger theory. Dunning implicitly retains the assumption that the MNE incurs additional costs of doing business abroad. But

> this assumption is no longer crucial because these costs are simply one component of the overall cost of integrating activities in different countries, and it is only the overall cost that is crucial to the theory. Likewise it is unnecessary to retain the postulate that an MNE possesses an ownership advantage such as a superior technology because the benefits of internalization are themselves sufficient, in principle, to outweigh the costs of internalization and so make integrated operations profitable.

Still, the difference between these theories is not as great as it may seem from this quotation. Casson instead transforms an explanatory factor in Dunning's theory to a postulate in his theory. The strategic factor is retained as a condition for successful internalization. Internalization theory instead builds more directly on Coase (1937), or on a more general transaction-cost theory.

4. Larsson (1989) provides examples of information controls of other types of institutions, e.g. 'personality' among friends, 'genes' within the clan, or ideology within political movements.
5. Cf. Williamson (1985, chapter 6).

3. Group Organization

The organizational structure of a transnational concern as a whole has a decisive impact on regional as well as local strategies, for example on strategies of establishment. In this chapter, the question of how a group, or TNC, is organized is taken up and six main types of organization are examined. As will be discussed, traditional studies of processes of internationalization tend to be too narrow, failing to adequately consider the organization of such processes or activities. In this chapter, the organization of internationalization processes is focused upon, how the geographical organization gradually takes form and is institutionalized when the regional activities reach a certain momentum being described. Among the TNCs that were studied, the existence of a regional organization of some kind was very common. When regional activities had become stabilized, the regional organization tended to be maintained, although a greater decentralization often occurred concomitantly. The view of internationalization which is adopted is thus a broad one, involving the consideration of a TNC's business strategies and its multinational organizational structure.

The results of the present study show in accordance with the findings of, for example, Stopford and Wells (1972) and Hedlund and Åhman (1984), that product divisions and product companies are a form of international organization that developed fairly late, subsidiaries that were founded tending to be poorly integrated into the structure of the group and to become very independent during earlier stages of internationalization. With increasing international commitment and growing interest in the close management of such operations, an international division was sometimes created within a group. Later, when international business had outgrown domestic business, the structure of the whole group tended to change so as to be centred on international operations, a global divisional structure taking form. As also shown below, the early divisionalized structure, which allowed market companies considerable independence within the framework of the global product organization to which they belonged, gradually changed, the control of such subsidiaries becoming more formalized and their being bound more closely to the product divisions/companies.[1] This is a matter which is also discussed in Chapter 4.

MAJOR GLOBAL ORGANIZATIONAL STRUCTURES

The analysis of the structure of the various groups is based on the organizational principles applying to the transnational M-form taken up in Chapter 2, TNCs being viewed as economic institutions. Like other governance forms, the transnational M-form represents a broad category of ways in which transactions can be organized. The major principles for the internal organization of transactions employed in economic institutions of the transnational corporation type provide various constraints on, as well as possibilities for, the organization involved, much in the same way as external governance forms constrain industrial marketing and purchasing strategies. In this chapter, six main organizational structures are compared, a deeper analysis of them being presented in Chapters 4, 5 and 6, where the local organization of TNCs is focused upon.

As discussed earlier, the distinction is made between three main types of interests within the organization of a TNC. Two of these have to do with the spatial aspect (which distinguishes a TNC from a uninational corporation), namely global interests and local interests (a regional organization providing a special way of organizing local interests). The third major type of interests, referred to here as company-wide interests, concerning the company in its entirety, is of a type found in all companies. Whereas global and local interests are parochial, company-wide interests involve the common interests of the firm. Such interests are assumed to be represented by group management (GM), which obtains its mandate from the company board, or ultimately from the shareholders and from other stakeholders. Company-wide interests can be considered as the overriding interests of a TNC. Thus, the organization structure, the various types of information control, behavioural control, output control and input control can be seen as ultimately favouring these interests, for example through controlling parochial interests so as to prevent these from getting out of hand or conflicting too strongly with company-wide interests (preventing suboptimization).

From earlier research on the organization of TNCs it can be concluded that the importance of global and local interests varies with the degree of internationalization of a TNC. At earlier stages in the development of an international organization, global interests may be weak. An organization consisting of an international division within an otherwise functionally organized company is more likely to favour local interests at the expense of the global interests, the major conflicts then being with the functional departments. At later stages, when the company has gained greater international experience and operates more on a worldwide scale, the trade-off between the three types of interests may vary with the form of organization of the TNC. Global interests tend to dominate in a worldwide product organization, since the entirety of the firm is organized in accordance with such interests. Most TNCs classified as having an 'international organization' seem to be organized in this way (Bartlett and Ghoshal, 1989). On the whole, such a TNC represents a partly centralized, partly decentralized organization, focus being placed on the middle management. In a regional organization it is the other way around, such an organization being dominated by local interests. This is typical of 'the multinational organization form' (Bartlett and Ghoshal, 1989). The international matrix type organization, in turn, takes about equal account of both these types of interests. In the TNCs that were studied, global interests tended usually to be organized in terms of product, whereas the organization of local interests was based on a strong customer orientation, the interests of this sort being represented by the sales companies. The main organizational task was to balance local and global interests as efficiently as possible from the perspective of company-wide interests. Such an organization can be seen as resembling the 'glocalized' 'transnational organization', one that is both global and local at the same time (Bartlett and Ghoshal, 1989). The 'transnational organization', in contrast, is much more of a multi-dimensional organization than either 'the global product organization' or 'the formal matrix organization' are. This is a matter considered in detail below in connection with examining the 'multidimensional organization' type.

A major organizational principle of the transnational M-form is the trade-off made between global integration and local responsiveness. This can be seen as mainly the balancing of global interests, as represented primarily by the product companies, with local interests, as represented by the market companies. In this way, a hierarchical decomposition principle is satisfied and both local and global effectiveness are promoted. Such a trade-off is illustrated by a comparison of the six group organizational structures represented in the study. These structures can be distinguished primarily in terms of the vertical organizational dimension, namely the relation between a manufactured product and its geographical markets. A horizontal dimension is present in addition to this vertical one, concerning how the various products and their markets are integrated. The grouping of organizational structures in this chapter reflects an assumption made that there are several potentially efficient structures and not simply one optimal structure, due to there being a varied environment that provides differing prerequisites for the reduction of transaction costs.

Most of the transnational corporations researched here were ones that were divisionalized. Four major decentralized group structures can be distinguished. The focus of the presentation here is on small market companies in what from a European perspective are distant markets. Thus, the local/regional aspect of global organization is emphasized, especially in Chapters 5 and 6.

Global Product Organization

Eleven of the TNCs studied have a global product organization with a basic structure of the type shown in Figure 3.1, although one of these

Figure 3.1 Global product organization

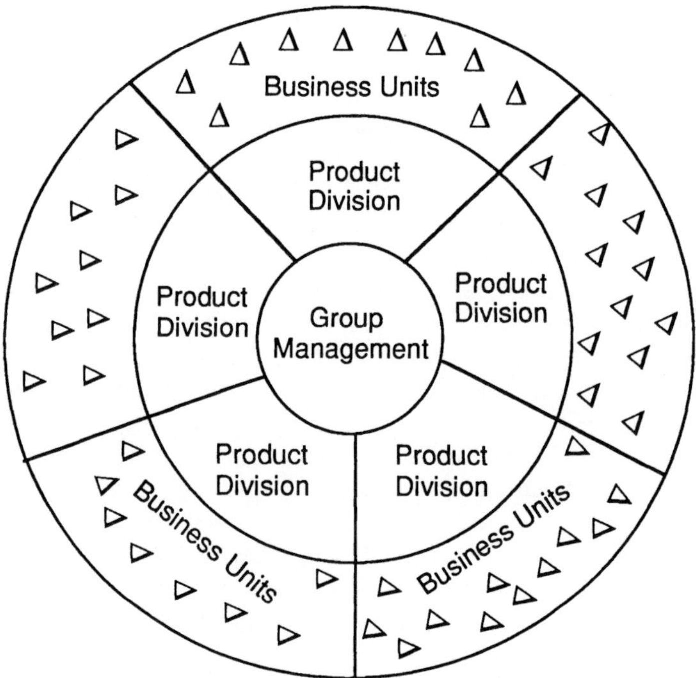

TNCs (see below) is in the process of change from this type of organization to one of a multi-dimensional type. When the global integration of a TNC is mainly based on the product dimension, the organizational structure tends to be centred around the product companies. This involves a subordination of the local dimension and of the concern for local customers to the global product dimension. Product aspects and technical aspects are more important in such TNCs, which often are producers of technologically sophisticated products, than is adaptation to the local markets (Hedlund, 1984, p. 119). Nevertheless, an efficient coordination of global product interests and of local interests does increase the TNC's competitiveness.[2] The efficiency of such a multi-centred organization is based in particular on the technological core and on asset-advantage factors. Efficiency is also based on transaction advantages from which the corporation's global competitive strength is partly derived. According to transaction-cost theory, transactions are economical to internalize in such a case, both typical asset advantage factors and transaction advantages resulting in low transaction costs. An organization of this sort is referred to in the book as a global product organization. It is similar to what Bartlett and Ghoshal (1989) call 'the international organization'.

The global product division structure is designed to reduce information costs by supporting the global decision-making in connection with a particular product or product group. Such an organizational structure also reduces enforcement costs through hierarchical vertical control of the implementation of decisions concerning local transactions. The formal authority of the product companies over the market companies tends to control both local decision-making and implementation, although biases in the two-way information flow between local and global units may complicate such control and increase transaction costs. If this formal vertical authority also allows the product companies to control conflicts between global and local interests, bargaining costs are often reduced. However, this is not always the case, since efficiency based on the favouring of global interests in decision making and in local activities may be achieved at the expense of product adaptation to the local conditions and of customized marketing, resulting in conflicts between global and local interests. Product companies may be unwilling to accept their subsidiaries' making and implementing decisions that fail to conform with global objectives. This can lead to inefficiency caused by sub-optimization. Such a situation can be remedied by reorganising the structure of controls so that transaction costs are reduced.

A global product organization is a late form of worldwide organizational structure. The changeover from primarily multi-domestic competition to far greater global competition affects the long-term competitive position of a TNC and consequently its major goals. A certain integration of operations on the various local markets becomes essential for such a company's international competitiveness. Although earning rents on proprietary assets through internalization is still important for the company, its competitiveness becomes increasingly dependent upon the firm-specific advantages of common governance. Just as it was earlier, internalizing the marketing of goods produced from proprietary assets is more economical than externalizing it. At the same time, the company's efficiency can be improved by actively co-ordinating the use of its assets throughout the world. Special assets are also created by the company gaining experience in how to accomplish this. Thus, internal organization has two types of ownership advantages for the company: asset advantages and transaction advantages. Environmental changes affect transaction cost patterns. The earlier trade-off between the three major types of transaction costs becomes inefficient. A new organizational structure is created and, with this, a new mixture of internal controls, as compared with the mother-daughter organization (see below) from which it often stemmed. Such an organizational change should result in a reduction in information and enforcement costs, but at the same time in a rise in bargaining costs.

In a global product organization of this sort, the market company reports directly to the product company or its management, which in turn reports to the management of the group. In such an organizational form, control of the market companies becomes more formalized and they become more closely linked with the product companies. This often means their independence being reduced as compared with the mother-daughter type organization. Ideally, every one of the market companies of the concern should answer to only one of the product companies, creating direct links between these units. However, this is often inefficient, particularly for companies operating in small markets in which the volume of business is insufficient for establishing more than one market company. As a consequence, individual subsidiaries of this sort frequently are representatives for more than one product company. The problem here of balancing vertical and horizontal integration can be solved in various ways. One way is to divide or slice the market company's organization up in accordance with the structure of the group's product companies. In such a mixed company each 'slice' answers to its product company. This possibility is illustrated in Figure 3.2. Another possibility is to link the market company with its major product company and let it serve as an agent for the others.

Figure 3.2

(a) 'Sliced up' global product organization

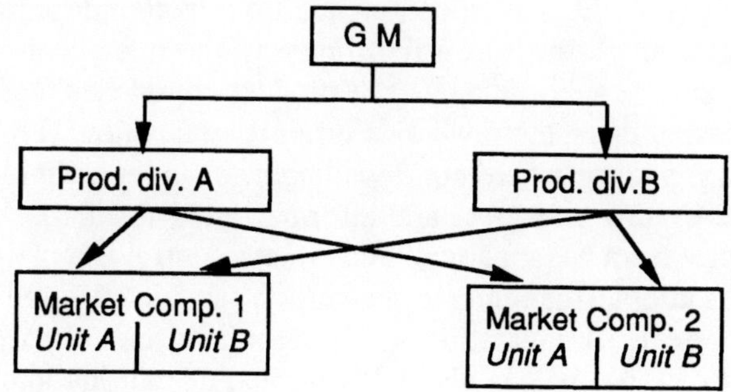

(b) Mother-daughter organization

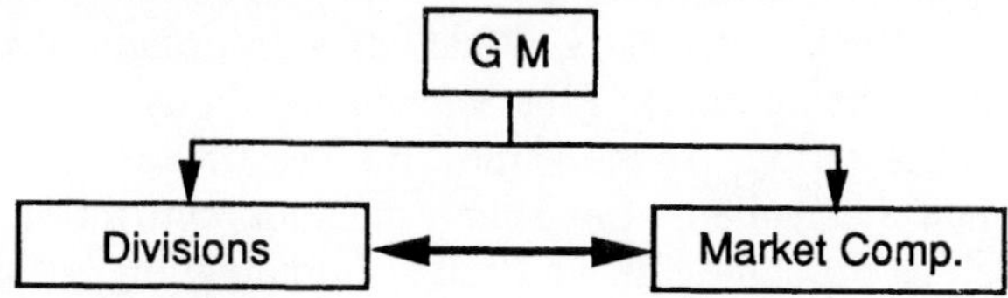

(c) Regional organization

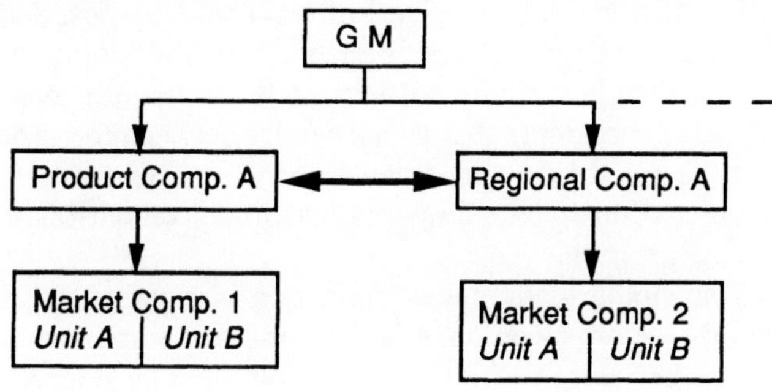

Mother-daughter Organization

A more traditional organizational form for a TNC is one in which local market interests are stronger than global product interests and the organization is of a more purely geographic character. This has been termed a 'mother-daughter' organization because of the marked importance of a direct relation between the 'mother' company and the 'daughter' firms located around the world. In a traditional organization of this type, the market companies are largely independent in the sense that, although they are subordinate to the management of the group, they are not subordinate to the product companies (see Figure 3.2). In the earlier days, there were no product companies. TNCs were not very diverse and they were not divisionalized, as for example along product lines. Control was loose and informal, and subsidiaries were controlled directly from headquarters. Such direct control is a major characteristic of the mother-daughter organization, and it is found irrespective of whether the organization is divisionalized or not. An organizational form of this sort has also been termed a 'multinational organization' (Bartlett and Ghoshal, 1989) or a 'loose federation' (Bartlett, 1986).

Whereas a global product organization sacrifices local responsiveness, a mother-daughter organization promotes it, favouring the integration of local needs on a global basis. Information costs are reduced by full use being made of the informational advantages of a decentralized organization. At the same time, as already discussed, if global aspects are considered important, the suboptimization that results can be seen as producing an inefficient organization, yielding high information costs from the perspective of the global organization as a whole. When the need for coordination within the TNC is slight, the mother-daughter organization is efficient. Transaction costs are reduced through decisions being decentralized, through the implementation of decisions being left to local subsidiaries, and through there being a low degree of control generally. At the same time, there is the risk of high bargaining costs in such an organizational structure. The costs for bargaining that is carried out between the product companies and the market companies tend to increase when the authority of the product companies is low and performance controls through transfer pricing are employed.

The mother-daughter organization is a rather 'primitive' form of worldwide organization, one that has been employed primarily during the earlier stages of internationalization. The interwar period of the twenties and thirties, for example, tended to be characterized by a multi-domestic pattern of competition developed on a country by country basis with little coordination or multinational control being required (Dunning, 1988a; Martinez and Jarillo, 1989).

From a competitive point of view, a mother-daughter organization is chiefly oriented towards earning rent on proprietary assets, and thus achieving the 'classical' firm-specific asset advantages of being a TNC. This organizational form can be seen as involving first, the motive to earn rent of this sort in as many markets as possible, and second, the advantages of organizing resource transfer internally rather than by way of the market. The marketing of the company's assets is adapted to local conditions, making the organization a loose network of units. Under the conditions of competition being multi-domestic, this organizational form yields very low transaction costs.

The mother-daughter type of organization was not found in its pure form in any of the groups that were studied. Nevertheless, even though *Wear and Tear*'s organization in the home country is divisionalized, for example, all its sales subsidiaries abroad are rather independent and are directly subject to group management. Thus, this organization can be classified as a mother-daughter organization. For a few of the other groups there are also vestiges of this organizational form in parts of the group. In SEA, various of the TNC's' subsidiaries possess a high degree of independence, reporting not to the product divisions but directly to group management. Also, control of the subsidiaries in the region tends to be rather informal (Hedlund and Åhman, 1984). Most decisions are decentralized to the market units, since it is often too inefficient for group management to be involved directly, although the latter does make clear certain key objectives. Despite, in a formal sense, being subordinate to group management, the majority of the contacts within the group take place directly between the product companies and the market companies, annual price agreements often being made in separate negotiations of this sort, which form the basis of the budgets.

Regional Structures

An organizational structure involving highly separate regional structures can be seen as very similar to that of the mother-daughter type, since it is decentralized along geographic lines and has many of the same characteristics. However, it is a simpler organizational type since it is only diversified in a geographical sense, and in terms of regions, rather than in terms of the markets of individual countries. There is thus a regional layer located between group management and management of the local subsidiaries, and a kind of divisionalized organization along geographical lines.

A purely geographic type of organization is found in four of the TNCs: *Pills*, *Specmat*, *Explo* and *Pacmat*. *Pacmat* differs from the general pattern of divisionalized organization analysed above in that it is a functionally organized corporation with an international division. The company has a rather simple form of organization, since it sells only one main type of product. Its degree of internationalization is very high, the degree of decentralization within its international division likewise being high and most of the market companies reporting directly to the divisional head office in Europe.

Geographic hybrids

Although in most of the TNCs that were studied, the product dimensions tend to dominate the organization, in a few cases the geographical dimension is so strong that the organizational form can be classed as hybrid. However, it is only in one of three separate hybrid forms that are described, namely case 2 below, that the geographical aspect is so strong that geographic interests are placed on an equal footing with product interests. The organizational hybrids all involve special adaptations being made to the particular market conditions in the Third World and in Eastern Europe. The three major combinations of geographic organization and product organization that were found in the study are the following:

1. An international division being embedded within a global product structure. Such a hybrid structure was originally found in two of the TNCs that were studied. It has been replaced in the one case, however, by a more pure form of global product organization, and in the other by a more pure two-dimensional organizational form. As the structure was originally, small market companies, often operating in various largely marginal markets, reported to an international division. These companies were represented by a common unit high within the group organization. If, as in the case of these two groups, most of the business conducted is with the product companies, there is little power that can be exerted over these market companies in any formal way via the international unit. The fact that this part of the worldwide organization became too complicated to be readily manageable led, in the case of these two TNCs, to abolition of the international division.

2. Regional companies being found alongside product companies. This hybrid represents a rather strong type, or independent form, of geographical organization (see Figure 3.2). The existence of regional companies here means that the group structure has been incorporated into the separate firms of the group, all of which answer to the parent company, which is organized as a holding company. The relations between the various regional and product companies within the group are market-like and are governed more by internal price than by authority. Depending on their size and location, market companies belong either to a regional or to a product company. A consequence of this is that separate regional company structures are formed within the framework of the group.
3. A mother-daughter organizational form existing alongside product companies. This hybrid form was discussed above as being a transitional type of organization in the process of changing from being a mother-daughter to being a global product organization. Specific circumstances dictate the mother-daughter organization being retained in certain parts of the organization, mainly in small markets situated far from the home base.

The last two types of hybrid organizations will be analysed in greater detail in Chapter 5.

Centralized Organization

The direct opposite of the two decentralized forms of organization described above – those of mother-daughter organization and regional structures type – is to be found in the centralized organization, one in which strategic decisions are taken at the top and are implemented in the subsidiaries. An international group of this sort, in which a strong coordination of the subsidiaries occurs at the top, is one said by Bartlett and Ghoshal (1989) to have a 'global organization' and by Bartlett (1986) to have a 'centralized hub'. According to these authors, Japanese TNCs, in which global interests and the worldwide interests coincide, are the archetype of this organizational form. Since such a centralized organization is the antithesis of the mother-daughter type organization, its disadvantages are also of the opposite sort. An organization that only promotes global efficiency can become unresponsive to local interests. Also, decisions that are taken far from the markets may become inefficient. In addition, an overload of information can occur at the top, something which is a well-known phenomenon.

Strong hierarchical control may not be able to control internal conflicts. This can lead to an increase in the costs of bargaining and of implementing decisions, which in turn can increase enforcement costs. However, the literature available suggests that the very strong corporate culture of Japanese TNCs, which emphasizes input control being achieved through socialization, may limit the occurrence of higher transaction costs. On the whole, the individual Japanese company (kaisha) or group of companies (keiretsu) seem very much a function of Japan as a country and of the specific institutions prevailing there, for example, those of the market organization, of authority, of control systems, and of employment and personal practices (Whitley, 1992).

No example of such a centralized organizational form was found in the present study.

Matrix Organization

A fifth form is that of the matrix organization. It has a balance between two separate dimensions, usually the product and the geographical dimensions. Such an organization commonly involves two parallel hierarchies, one based on the organization's global product responsibility and the other on its responsibilities regarding local markets, the two intersecting at certain points. A grid organization of this sort can be assumed to be a particularly efficient solution to the problems of many of the present-day TNCs. In many industries, international competition is now both global and local, something which seems to often call for an integrative matrix type of organization in which there is a balance between local responsiveness and global integration.[3] For such an organization, the geographic dimension is as important as the product dimension.

More than in the case of the other organization forms considered here, the hierarchical efficiency of this organizational form originates from the common governance of interrelated activities worldwide. With the establishment of a market position in most local markets of interest and an increase in global competition, the growth of a TNC comes more from its increased international involvement as a whole than from its initial entry into new geographic markets. It is vital that synergistic advantages be utilized, for example, and that production and marketing be rationalized. The advantages of common governance are greater and more sophisticated here than in the case of the global product organization, integration being based both on global and local interests rather than on global interests alone. The internal controls are more complex.

For a matrix organization it is particularly difficult to separate asset advantages from transaction advantages, the two tending to intermingle. In developing a new proprietary asset, for instance, it is essential to assess its potential for creating advantages in terms of common governance, through considering such questions as in what part of the world it should be manufactured and how production of it should be integrated with its sale in the various local markets, as well as how the new transactions involved can be integrated with the previous transactions of the TNC. Accordingly, whether such new activities should be internalized or externalized depends on the transaction costs that would be involved. An internalizing of transactions through the setting up of a subsidiary may be undertaken, for example, so as in part to avoid the transaction costs connected with appropriating the returns obtained from proprietary assets, and in part to take advantage of the gains connected with integrating these activities with those of the rest of the TNC. Expressed differently, there are advantages of internalization both for a particular geographical unit as achieved through specific import-substitution or a certain supply-oriented investment, for example, and for the parent system as a whole through such matters as taking advantage of economies of scale and scope (integration). A competitive advantage based on such a combination of asset and transaction-cost advantages may be difficult to achieve outside the own organization. Since the achieving of an intricate mixture of assets or advantages of this sort is hard to lift out separately from the overall activities of the group and to transfer to some outside organization there can be said under such conditions to be a low degree of substitutability between the market and the own hierarchy, unless there should exist a 'market' for suitable firms.

A major problem for the matrix organization is the built-in conflict between global product interests and local interests. It is assumed to be possible, through negotiation and through the utilization of many different sorts of subtle and informal control mechanisms, to reduce the bargaining costs this conflict results in. However, the conflict also generates information within the organization which can be used for control purposes. In the process of such conflict, local market interests and global product interests may be reconciled. This can reduce the information costs required for decision making. If organizational controls are able to strike a balance between the two sets of interests, both global effectiveness and local effectiveness may be increased, resulting in a lowering both of the information costs needed for decision making and of the enforcement costs required for implementing decisions. However, if the matrix organization leads instead to fights over domains and to unclear authority (the two-boss problem), confusion is created, rendering control more difficult. All three types of transaction cost may rise dramatically then, making it more efficient to replace the matrix organization with some other type of organization.

This sensitivity of the matrix organization to high transaction costs may be a major reason for its unpopularity. In fact, none of the TNCs that were studied were found to have such a formal matrix organization. This is not surprising in view of the experience the TNCs tended to have had with this organizational form, a form which had become increasingly unpopular due to the unmanageability of its problems of control. The hybrid organization presented above, consisting both of regional companies and of product companies, could be viewed as a kind of matrix organization due to these two main types of companies having an equal standing within the global organization. However, such an organization does not represent a formal matrix. Rather, it involves quite a different solution to the conflict between the two major dimensions in the international organization of a TNC.

Other matrix dimensions

Another kind of matrix-like organization, one that was found in one of the TNCs (*Weldprod*), involves market companies being directly subordinate both to the management of the group as in the mother-daughter type organization, and to separate product companies, as in the global product organization, equal weight being given to the authority of both. There is a dual command structure, which can be either an advantage or a disadvantage of this organizational type, depending upon how the system works. This type of organization results in less independence for the market companies since they become directly controlled by worldwide interests.

The Multidimensional Organization

The unpopularity of the formal matrix organization might be seen as a hindrance to any general tendency developing to give equal importance to the product and geographic dimensions in the worldwide organization of a TNC. However, the relation between the two does not have to be organized formally in terms of a matrix. A deliberate and formal linkage of them seems to force conflicts out in the open and to blur the lines of command. Most of those TNCs that tried out such an organizational form have subsequently changed to a more clear-cut structure, chiefly that of the global product organization. Also, these two major dimensions can coexist in an organization of the hybrid form. In the latter, however, they are not hierarchically connected, only one of the two dimensions being valid for any given part of the organization. Indeed, the five organizational forms mentioned thus far have in common their being one-dimensional. Each of them is based on one major strategic perspective: for the global product organization technology is the main competitive factor; for the mother-daughter organization and regional structures form it is market adaptation (closeness); for the centralized organization it is global efficiency; and for the matrix organization it is a combination of either local/central or global product/group management.

Except for the various hybrid forms, they also have in common that all parts of the organization are treated in the same way. According to Bartlett and Ghoshal (1989), organizational forms of the types just referred to represent too simple a solution to the present and future needs of a TNC, what is required being rather that such a worldwide organization be multidimensional and more differentiated, since several of these strategic perspectives are each important in their own right and should be employed in accordance with the situation. The various one-dimensional forms can also be seen as placing too much emphasis on formal structure. A combination of different strategic perspectives requires that the organization be more open and that informal aspects of organization be given greater weight. Bartlett and Ghoshal (1989) call such a form of organization 'transnational', characterizing it as representing an ideal for the future organization of TNCs. It involves such organizational principles as those of complexity, differentiation and integration, 'glocalization', a network type of organization being found, and both complex and flexible cooperation as well as coordinatory processes being emphasized. Corporate culture, vision, and human resource management are seen as critical ingredients (due to the focus on the individual). Such an organization form, as evident in Figure 3.3, can be seen as representing a breaking up of the sort of global product organization depicted in Figure 3.1. The focus here on the market companies is illustrated for one of these units, shown connected both horizontally to other market companies and vertically to different product divisions, as well as to group management. A specific example of this organizational form is presented in the next section.

Figure 3.3 Multidimensional organization

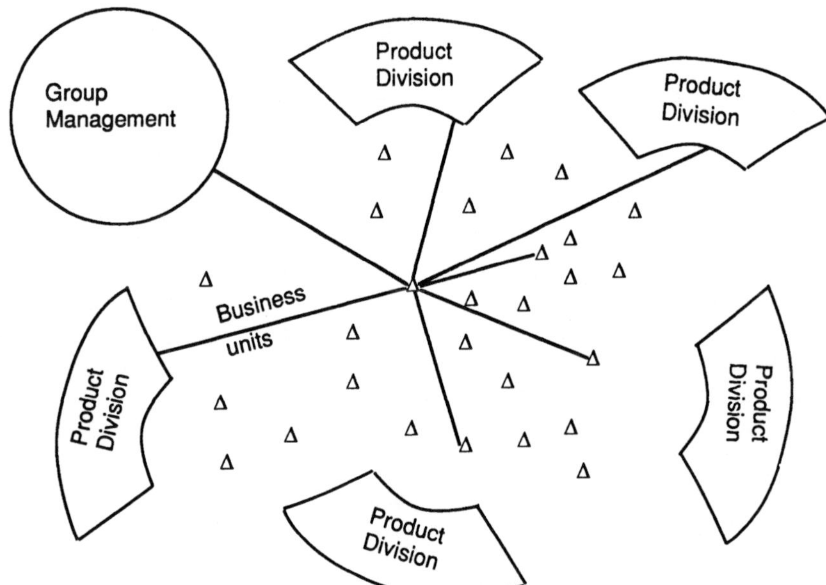

Example of a multidimensional organization

One of the TNCs studied (*Telecom*) is in the process of changing to a multidimensional organization form. This TNC has experienced the following major problems connected with an organizational form centred around global divisions:

1. Market orientation. Since a global product organization is mainly technology-driven, and the product-based technology originates at a high organizational level and flows through the company pipelines out into the market, there is the risk that the technology is not sufficiently adapted to the customer, thus causing national and regional responsiveness to become too low.
2. Horizontal communication. Since such an organization is vertically segmented, horizontal contacts are hampered. This can be a serious problem if the situation on the various local markets requires joint activities involving several product divisions due to the core competencies involved, for example in marketing and product development.

3. Control of the product divisions. The divisions in the global product organization may become too strong and develop their business in directions that are questionable or too risky as seen from the perspective of the group, control and coordination of the product divisions by group management thus being too weak.
4. Confusion among customers. Since in the global product organization there is no joint approach by the group, and since customers may therefore have to deal with several different representatives from the same group, they can readily become confused. This is of particular significance if the customer structure is highly concentrated.
5. High costs. The duplication of offices and functions in the global product organization may raise costs.

Such problems became acute for *Telecom*, due to such major environmental changes as deregulation, privatization, technological development, and the offering of new services, all of which gradually lead to markets becoming more fragmented and to increased competition. Since technological developments now occur in more regions than Europe alone, the TNC must increase its presence in these markets in order to survive.

Developments have also converged on one specific core competence for which *Telecom* has a first-mover advantage. In the old organization, informal horizontal communication took place between product divisions, especially in certain of the local markets such as those of Southeast Asia. Formal solutions to this lateral communication problem have not worked well, for example, the appointment of 'country co-ordinators' with the aim of achieving a more joint approach of business in the various regions. To really adapt to the major ongoing changes that occurred, and to retain its competitive edge, the company had to solve the major problems listed above. This could only be achieved by dissolving *Telecom*'s global product organization, the organization of the company as a whole opened up so as to facilitate both vertical and horizontal communication at all levels through removing any direct linkages between the product divisions and the subsidiaries. The subsidiaries were moved back to the 'mother-daughter' position by being assigned to group management. At the same time, some of their former independence was restored by increasing their competence and giving them full responsibility for all activities involving customers. They thus have full product-line responsibility and profit responsibility.

However, there is one major difference here as compared with the traditional organization form. This has to do with the role of the product divisions. These have been kept, but their role has changed from being hierarchical to being supportive. The product divisions are now supposed to jointly support the marketing activities of the subsidiaries so that these will be able to offer customers *Telecom*'s full competence and resources. Directives are provided by the product divisions to market units regarding such matters as strategy, transfer price schemes, pricing and purchasing, at the same time as they have the responsibility for the coordination and transfer of experience and know-how in matters of design, production, and quality. The business area management still has responsibility for worldwide results. This involves two major roles: global product line management and the coordinated development of technology, methods, systems and core systems components. At the same time, the role of group management is changed, since the overall activities of the group are now all represented at this level. This affects strategic planning, business development and the coordination of different functions. The product divisions and the local companies reach mutual agreements on strategy and on important operational matters, the group management being involved here and being responsible for controlling that such agreements are reached with the best results possible for *Telecom* as a whole. The group management acts as a single body, its members being given specific responsibilities that may change from time to time. The resources available from the various business areas are used to carry out the tasks decided on at the group level. Management teams are established at the product division and local company levels so as to increase coordination. Each unit has a total profit responsibility.

Various of the major aims in creating the new organization are as follows: to achieve a more boundary-free organization through the broadening of communications; to come closer to customers and have more time for them; and to increase flexibility and quality and, with this, profit. The organization of the group focused on the market end of things, where a mix aimed at that specifically reflects the local market situation. The structure here is modelled, in so far as possible, in accordance with the global organizational structure, although this is difficult in such a decentralized organization in which local responsiveness is so important. The more centralized an organization is, the easier it is to extend its global organizational structure to different parts of the organization.

One major consequence of the organizational evolution just described is that the differentiation of *Telecom*'s structure is much increased. Growth in the future will doubtlessly take place primarily within the company's foreign markets and not within the home country.

CONCLUSIONS

Five major types of global organizational structure were found to apply to the TNCs that were studied: the global product organization, the mother-daughter organization, the regional structures form, the matrix organization, and the multidimensional organization. All of them can be inferred from, and related to, the transnational M-form discussed in Chapter 2. Organizational structure and other controls considered here can be viewed as means for reducing information, bargaining and enforcement costs, aspects which are also affected by uncertainty, opportunism and the other factors included in the transaction-cost model.

NOTES

1. For a summary of TNC organization and growth, see Caves (1982, chapter 3). See also Milton-Smith (1985, pp. 12-13) for a summary of Japanese experience in this area.
2. See Porter (1986) for example.
3. Recently, a number of much publicized books on the management of large TNCs discuss how this should be done within an integrative transnational organization, suggesting how very complicated management in this area has become (see, for example, Prahalad and Doz, 1987, and Bartlett and Ghoshal, 1989). In these and other publications based on the Harvard Business School research tradition, these main organizational forms are given other labels. The mother-daughter organization is referred to as the decentralized federation model or as the multinational organization, the global product organization is called the international organization or the coordinated federation, and the multidimensional organization is termed the integrative network model or the transnational organization. (See, for example, Bartlett, 1986; Ghoshal and Bartlett, 1988; Bartlett and Ghoshal, 1989; Doz, 1986.)

4. Establishment Processes and Organization of Transactions in Southeast Asia

Processes of internationalization within TNCs appear, at least in the earlier stages, to emerge in a stepwise manner, companies committing themselves to internationalization through a gradual learning process. The costs for information search as well as the perceived risks are higher than in domestic investments (Caves, 1982, pp. 68-73). Companies tend, therefore, to first establish themselves in markets that are geographically and culturally proximate and to gradually increase their international involvement starting with agents in foreign countries and moving on to the establishment of sales companies and later on to manufacturing companies there (Johanson and Wiedersheim-Paul, 1975).

> Casual evidence on other source countries confirms the general impression that the bulk of their foreign investment go where the transactional and information-cost disadvantages are least: Japan to Southeast Asia ... Australia to New Zealand ... Sweden to neighboring European countries and the Unites States... France to French-speaking lands and adjacent European countries. (Caves, 1982, p. 64)

Most of the direct investments in Canada and Australia from the UK between 1945 and 1960 have been shown to have followed such a pattern (Dunning, 1988a, p. 110).

One can ask whether this is a process encompassing the entire globalization of multinational firms. Do investments in geographically and culturally very distant markets follow this pattern? In a study of Swedish investments in Japan, for example, Hedlund and Kverneland (1985, pp. 22-3) state that,

> the experience of Swedish firms in Japan suggests that establishment and growth strategies in foreign markets are changing towards more direct and rapid entry modes than those implied by theories of gradual and slow internationalization processes. Around half of the companies investigated went directly from a sales agent to manufacturing in Japan, rather than taking the route over a sales subsidiary.

Johanson and Mattsson (1987), examining firms with varying degrees of multinationalization, suggest that gradual, step-by-step processes are mainly characteristic of the early stages of internationalization. They maintain that, in companies of broad experience, globalization is largely the result of international strategies decided on for the company generally, making the processes neither gradual nor slow.

The aim in this chapter is to illustrate how internationalization processes for the major activities of TNCs, namely sales, production and purchasing, develop in geographically and culturally distant markets. The matter of how the TNCs that were studied produce and purchase within the geographical areas where they conduct business is an important one to consider for gaining an adequate understanding of how such TNCs are organized. The processes involved are illustrated for various of the cases, although the conclusions presented are based on the empirical material as a whole.

A traditional model of internationalization processes concerns a TNC's strategies of entry and of becoming established. Since the overall structure of a TNC has a decisive impact on its basic 'establishment' strategy, and thus on its local organization and strategy as well, this relation between the strategies followed and the major types of group organization dealt with in the previous chapter are analysed here. The adopting of the strategies in question is interpreted in part from the perspective of transaction cost.

One major issue taken up is whether such entry strategies are the result of increased internationalization or whether it is the other way around. This issue was raised by Johanson and Mattsson (1987), who argued that traditional internationalization processes such as depicted by Johanson and Wiedersheim-Paul (1975) are not valid for TNCs that have reached a certain level of internationalization. One type of company of this sort is 'the international among others' type with a high degree of internationalization, in particular as regards its market and production network. The ongoing actions of a company of this kind of long international experience tend to follow from its global strategies, which can be classified as intended strategies. Its involvement in major undertakings is generally swift and direct. A search and learning process in which internationalization more or less emerges, appears in these terms to have been largely replaced by strategies reached by a decision process characterized by planning.

The strategy formation expressed in models of gradual internationalization processes has many similarities of an emerging strategy. Many actions take place without being intended from the start, behavioural patterns that are internationally oriented often developing from the lower ranks within the company to only later be adopted as a general strategic posture. Firms of 'the international among others' type, would seem to have more deliberate global strategies than this. Their international experience makes it possible for them to formulate strategies from the start and then to implement them. They could be thought, at least, to plan their international activities to a greater degree than companies that tend generally to operate in accordance with a gradual internationalization model.

ESTABLISHMENT PROCESSES IN SOUTHEAST ASIA

The present findings suggest, however, that the matter is not as simple as this, that elements of a gradual internationalization model may indeed by found in the approach to SEA of the TNCs that were studied. The development of Asian operations in these TNCs can be summarized in terms of three different stages in the establishment chain. The first stage, called here the introductory stage, can start with salesmen from the parent company travelling to the area, this being followed by some kind of representation in the market, usually in the form of an agent or a resident salesman. The second stage involves the establishment of sales companies and the third stage the manufacturing operations. At the same time there are also examples of the simultaneous establishment of both major activities. The pattern selected is partly determined by the reasons for investing in manufacturing operations within the area. A regional concept is usually formed early and the companies managed from a regional centre. The establishment stage has been completed when the company's business in the area takes off. For some of the TNCs that were studied this manifested itself as a decentralization within the region of the operations that had been established. For others, the regional concept was deepened and broadened at the same time as the subsidiaries in the area were reorganized (see Chapters 5 and 6). The establishment process is shown schematically in Figure 4.1.

Stage One: The Introductory Phase

Pacmat started business in Asia very early on. The initial sale anywhere of the company's first piece of major equipment was in 1952, the first sale in Asia being in 1958. During the sixties,

Figure 4.1 The internationalization process

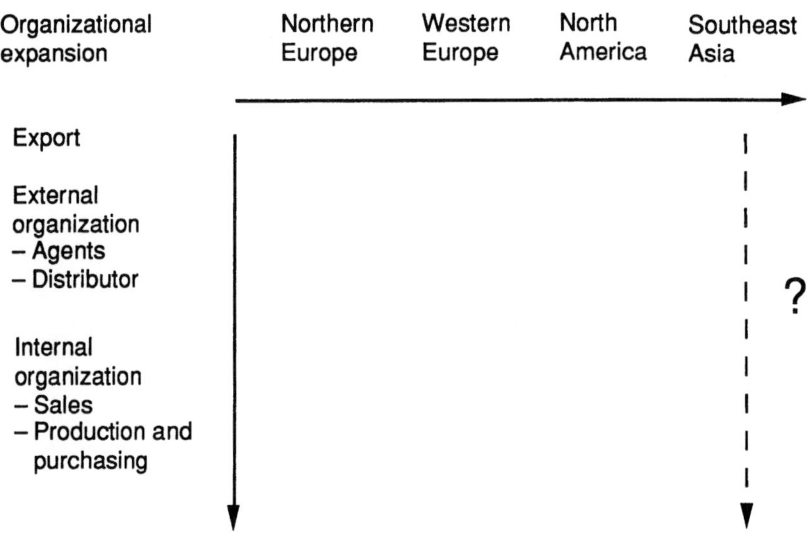

nevertheless, *Pacmat* kept a low profile in Asia, operations there being directed from Europe. There were agents for the company in various of the markets and salesmen from the European offices travelled there sometimes for periods of about a week, seeing a limited number of customers. The company's first permanent representation of its own in the region, involving a resident salesman who covered most of SEA, was established in 1970 in Kuala Lumpur.

Salesmen from *Food equipment* travelled in the area too, in the beginning sporadically. Both this company and *Conmine* were represented mainly then by agents. As regards *Pills*, Asian agents began to carry its first major success product in the 1960s. This led to the establishment of the company's first office in Singapore at the end of that decade.

Stage Two: The Sales Company Phase

The second stage in the development of international operations involves the establishment of sales companies. In the TNCs studied, a geographically-based organization was usually founded to control this stage of the establishment process, a regional centralization of various activities tending to take place.

Around 1975 the Far Eastern markets began to look more promising for *Pacmat* than they had earlier. A regional sales and service company for the Asian area was established in Hong Kong. Market companies were gradually formed between 1974 and 1982 in the various countries involved when turnover had reached a profitable level. Since close contacts with its customers are vital to *Pacmat*, it prefers being represented through its own agents. With the opening of a second regional office in Singapore in 1978, the responsibility of the Hong Kong office was limited to that of Northeast Asia. Between 1977 and 1980, market companies were established in the Philippines, Thailand, Taiwan, Malaysia and South Korea. In Indonesia a joint venture was established in 1982, since majority-owned subsidiaries are not allowed there. The periods of establishment were rather long, for example in Thailand taking three years. Salesmen had been visiting customers in that country ever since the beginning of the sixties. When *Pacmat* noticed the coming of a boom in 1977, it quickly established a market company there.

By 1982 *Pacmat* had established sales and service units in every Far Eastern country of interest except for Japan. The policy was to establish such units just before the market started to boom, although this did not succeed in all cases. When some of the then rather small number of potential customers commenced manufacturing and thus needed equipment, a potential became evident and a market unit was established.

Food equipment's first Southeast Asian subsidiary was established in Malaysia in 1962. Establishment of a sales company was spurred by the fact that Malaysia became within just a brief period of time the world's leading producer of palm-oil and *Food equipment* already had a minor piece of equipment that suited well the needs of this industry. By 1985 the company had supplied about 80% of all such equipment in use there, which was a unique experience. The boom was exceptionally strong for a time, the market share being very large and the profits high. This situation changed radically in 1982-3, when there was a sharp decline in production and in prices, leading to half of the sales volume disappearing within a very short time. In 1984 the situation stabilized somewhat through a restructuring of the Malaysian palm-oil industry.

Food equipment took its next major step in SEA at the beginning of the seventies, when a branch office of the Malaysian sales company was opened in Singapore. This later became a separate sales company and also became a regional office, first for most of the Far East and later for SEA. This Singapore company is also responsible for all the agents in the area. In 1983 a market company was started in Thailand, the earlier agent being bought up. *Food equipment* had then been operating in the country for about 20 years and had a contract with the agent that carried the whole range of the TNC's products. Although the agent had a short-term orientation and concentrated its business on the most profitable items, the relationship worked well for many years. However, with rising competition and very reduced sales, *Food equipment* decided to take it over.

The company's main organizational problem in the region was to bridge as effectively as possible the gap between the customers in SEA and the product manufacture in Europe. With an increasing number of customers some kind of own representation of the company soon became necessary. The larger number of customers in a vast region hard to traverse in many parts could not be handled competitively from Europe. Also, because of the customized marketing required, it was essential for the company to establish itself as close as possible to its final customers. The first step was to establish an office in Singapore in the mid-seventies, operations and various resources being moved there from Europe. However, the regional concept first started to take shape in 1980, a considerable rationalization of the business in Malaysia and Singapore being achieved.

Conmine established its first market company in the Philippines, which is an important mining area, in 1967. In the other SEA countries the company was represented by agents. *Conmine* began to invest heavily in the region as a whole in 1979, the establishment pace being speeded up. Locally responsive companies were formed in many of the countries of the region. However, the company's resources were not sufficient to permit investment in all of the countries, at the same time as investment in only one country at a time seemed too slow an alternative. Singapore served as a base for the penetration of the region, a sales company being founded there in 1979. In 1982 a market company was established in Malaysia and a joint venture in Indonesia. At about the same time, sales companies were also formed in Hong Kong, South Korea and Taiwan.

During this period of build-up, the new companies were supported by a group of specialists based in Singapore. The establishment period was managed from the sales company in Singapore, which took on a regional role during that phase. Through its agents, *Conmine* was informed early when the demand for its products began to increase. The market companies established were quite profitable. Some of them broke even after a year, and most of them after two years, as compared with the usual estimate of three years.

The sales of *Pills'* first major product had by the end of the 1960s grown to the stage where an office of its own was needed to control the agents in the area. One was established in Singapore, shortly after the establishment of an office in Japan. Over the years, particularly during the 1980s, the agents were largely replaced by the company's own sales offices.

Stage Three: Manufacturing and Purchasing

Manufacturing

Up to 1990, however, most of the TNCs studied had not yet established production in SEA (see Table 1.2). The companies investing in production there and their reasons for doing so are shown in Figure 4.2. The main reason for a company's not investing there, except for three of the cases, is that the markets are too small for an efficient utilization of economies of scale to be possible. In such small and far-off markets the combination of the minimum optimal scale needed for

Figure 4.2 Reasons for production in the ASEAN countries

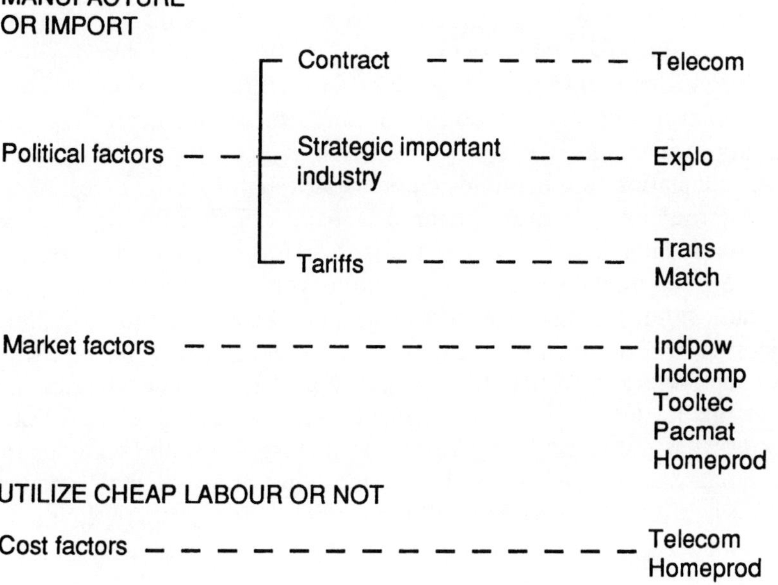

a plant and the low frequency of transactions is the main constraint to locating production there. Nevertheless, some of the TNCs did find it sensible to locate production in SEA for consumption there.

Growth in sales for *Pacmat*'s machines created a basis for the establishment of an Asian manufacturing unit for the input materials for these machines. Singapore was selected as the site for the unit, since Singapore possessed a large number of advantages: the country is an ASEAN member, and it has free capital movements, a small bureaucracy, no corruption and a good infrastructure. Its main drawback is the very small domestic market it has. Until the mid-1980s, materials produced there were distributed to all the South and East Asian markets, whereupon a second factory with a lower value-added level was established in Taiwan, followed by a third one in Korea a short time thereafter. These factories are linked with the main factory in Singapore through the major input material being delivered from this plant.

Food equipment began, when the regional concept had been institutionalized, to investigate possibilities for establishing regional production facilities, and in 1982 a joint venture for the manufacture of components, was formed in Indonesia.

The products produced by *Pacmat* and *Indcomp* are exported to other Asian countries. The aggregation of markets makes the frequency of transactions large enough for regional production to be profitable. Locating production regionally also makes it possible for the matter of lower transport costs to be taken advantage of. Generally speaking, an adequate market size can be considered a precondition for the investing in production facilities. High duties are a more doubtful reason for doing so, since these can easily change, making investments risky.

An adaptation to specific local demand through specific investments in customer relationships appeared to have affected the decision to produce locally in a few of the cases. For *Indpow*, the main reason for the local manufacturing of a certain type of minor equipment is not duties, but the fact that products have to be adapted to individual customer needs, which is best done in close contact with buyers, who visit the factory to inspect the product to arrange for changes that are to be made during the manufacturing process, and the like. Such flexibility is not possible in a European factory due to the high degree of standardization. Also, local manufacturing provides the company with a particularly good reputation since it creates local employment. A minor reason for local production in the case of *Indpow* is also the matter of transport costs, since most of the company's products are rather bulky.

In one case (*Telecom*), local production was demanded by the customer as a condition for buying the equipment. For this TNC, which sells major equipment that is technologically advanced, local production is often part of the offer to the local customer, the latter usually being a large public organization. In a way, local manufacturing serves as a ticket here for admission to the market, where the low duties levied on this high-priority industry only marginally influence decisions regarding location. The matter of where the production of the major equipment the company produces should be located is thus highly complex, influenced in particular by the combined consideration of transaction and production costs. Transaction costs can be reduced by moving production closer to customers. However, this spreading of manufacturing out to several smaller factories leads to an increase in production costs as compared with centralizing production to one or a few large factories. This does not mean that all the company's equipment sold in SEA is manufactured there. Indeed, the technologically most advanced parts are manufactured elsewhere and imported, the matter of production costs being particularly critical in such cases.

For *Telecom*, and also for most of the other TNCs involved, local manufacturing took place in small plants, these producing only a few of the company's products. In a few cases, political reasons, primarily tariffs, were decisive to producing locally. Surprisingly, the low labour costs of producing things locally hardly seemed to have been an important factor for any of these TNCs. Thus, they did not use SEA as a basis for lowering their production costs generally. Local production was more a result of investment in the market there than of the lower input costs this would involve. Production investments were based on regional market or local market expansion and were not made to rationalize the global manufacturing of the TNC.

Purchasing

With the establishment of production units in the region, it also became essential for purchasing activity to be anchored there for the buying of inputs to factory production and for the development and maintenance of local suppliers. The TNCs were also faced with new problems connected with the manufacturing of products, making purchasing particularly complicated. Whereas finished products had been bought from the home company earlier, intermediary products were now bought for the regional or local factory either from the home company or from outside suppliers.

As shown in Figure 4.3, the strategic purchasing options open to TNCs that already have plants in a region are either to import a product that is required or to buy it from local suppliers. As will be discussed below, the 'make' alternative is not of interest in the case of technology products that are too expensive to integrate backwards. Capacity products, in contrast, can be either produced in their own factory or bought from suppliers.[1] However, this latter product category does not appear to be a relevant one in SEA for the TNCs that were studied.

THE POST-ESTABLISHMENT PERIOD

With the launching of the factory in Singapore, *Pacmat*'s regional mandate was expanded to encompass business in the whole of the West Pacific rim except for Australia and Japan. The regional company also had a direct responsibility for sales in Malaysia, Singapore, Indonesia, India and Sri Lanka. However, at about the same time, a decentralization of market responsibility was introduced with the aim of winding up the work of the regional organization. By 1989 *Pacmat* had virtually achieved this goal, all the market companies except the one in Malaysia reporting directly to the head office in Europe. The overall regional office with its coordinating function had been closed down.

Food equipment initiated a regional decentralization in 1984 with the aim of improving its position. Technical knowledge and other resources were gradually transferred from the regional centre to the relatively new market units, even though special know-how and facilities for the more complicated products were largely kept in Singapore. The intention with decentralization was to come closer to customers and adapt business to local conditions and goals, at the same time as knowledge of local conditions at the regional office was increased.

In 1985 *Food equipment* acquired an already established position in off-shore industry through purchasing a company in Singapore which had subsidiaries in most Southeast Asian countries. This is an example, rare to the study, of a company buying itself a position in industry rather than building it up gradually through green-field investment.

Figure 4.3 Main make or buy options

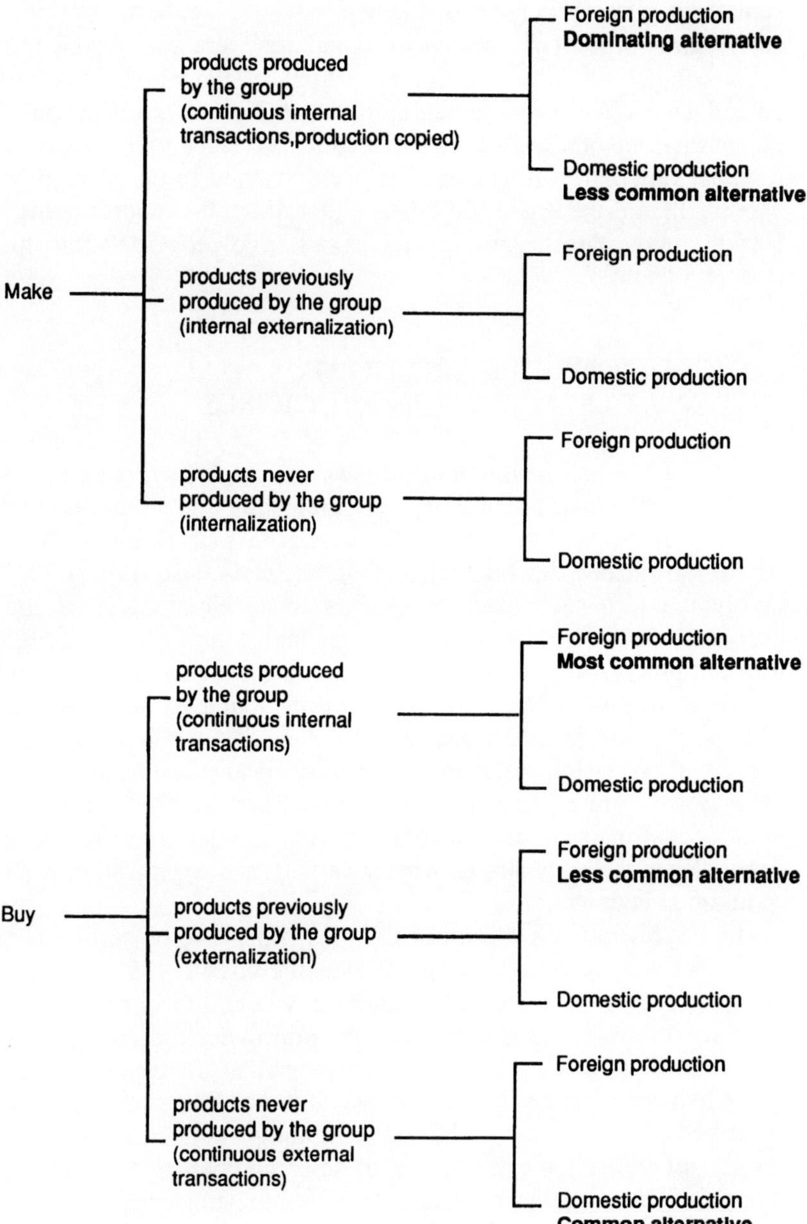

Conmine likewise began a decentralizing of common regional activities so as to make the market companies more independent, something which was not possible before the market basis for this was sufficient. Some of the specialist capacities were transferred to the sales companies, while others were kept in Singapore. Centrally-posted specialists provide the company with a flexibility that the rather small market companies are unable to finance individually. The regional function in Singapore has been changed to the managing of agents, being the main function rather than the coordinating of market units. The organizational issues involved are taken up in Chapters 5 and 6.

CONCLUSIONS REGARDING GRADUAL INTERNATIONALIZATION PROCESSES

A gradual internationalization process seems to have considerable validity for the investment in the geographically and culturally distant markets of SEA (Jansson, 1988; Lundgren and Hedlund, 1983). Although, during the later phases of internationalization a TNC's involvement in such markets appears to accelerate and its mode becomes more direct, a process of gradual commitment through a learning process appears to still be present. The assumptions a model of this sort involves seem to be present in Southeast Asian markets, which are at an informational and transactional disadvantage compared with West-European and North-American markets, at the same time as they are of only marginal importance to TNCs during the basic period of becoming established. An external organization predominates at the early stages, whereas an internal organization is most common at later stages.

The establishment pattern in SEA thus appears to be similar to the one described by Johanson and Wiedersheim-Paul (1975). It is an evolving process of incremental learning, where the commitment and the pace of investment increase with improved knowledge of the geographical area. This can also be interpreted as the psychic distance being reduced. The basic chain of events in becoming established, as described above, seems to be valid, although the second and third stages, involving the establishing of sales companies and manufacturing facilities, appear to sometimes be combined. A regional organization is usually formed during the establishment period, with the separate companies being managed from a regional centre. When the establishment period is over, a regional decentralization of operations that have been established sometimes takes place. The establishment of the Southeast Asian operations of the TNCs that were studied appeared to have been rather late compared with the other parts of their international networks. On the whole, the internationalization processes involving these markets seem to still be gradual and cautious.

At the same time the establishment of the market companies was sometimes more direct and took place without an agent for the company having been in the market prior to this. Lundgren and Hedlund (1983, p. 45), in a study of Swedish TNCs operating in SEA, found that the establishment of many sales companies surprisingly occurred in this direct way. In the present study, this was found to particularly be the case late in the regional establishment phase, when companies had gained considerable knowledge concerning the region and there was strong and rapid economic growth in most markets of the region. Many subsidiaries 'mushroomed' during the late seventies and early eighties. By that time, a considerable number of TNCs had some form of presence in the area, obtaining direct contact with the markets and building up a knowledge of the region which came in handy when business increased. This illustrates the importance of timing investments in the region correctly in terms of market growth.

The gradual increase in the involvement in SEA of the TNCs that were studied, and their cumulative insight into business in the region are in accordance with a theory of gradual internationalization processes, particularly if the establishment process is viewed from a regional perspective rather than from the perspective of the individual country. Assuming the establishment chain to be followed by every firm in every country at the same pace would indeed be too strict an interpretation of such a model.

In some cases, neither sales companies nor production companies were established following the introductory stage, specifically in countries in which foreign investments of this sort were not allowed, as in Indonesia for example. In such countries, TNCs continue to be represented by agents or distributors, the property rights of the foreign firms there being restricted by the broader institutional framework.

The results of the study also emphasized the importance of a TNC's changing its representation to some other form than that by agents as business conditions change. Flexibility is a key aspect of external organization of this type, since investments in specialist structures are low, yielding low switching costs. 'Gentlemen's agreements' are quite common. These relationships involved represent bilateral governance and thus lack the formal contracts that govern relationships under trilateral governance (see below). However, there is a certain bonding between the parties. The TNCs participate in the selling of complicated industrial products, since the agents tend to be lacking in technical knowledge, although the agents invest in certain transaction-specific equipment, for example in service facilities. This reduces transaction costs, where this includes losses due to moral hazard. An important aspect of external organization is thus to balance transaction-specific investments against flexibility.

Another variation found from the average pattern concerns sales companies and agents of a particular TNC operating in parallel within a given country. A TNC sometimes retains an agent despite having established a sales company of its own. Transactions are divided up then between the two, the agent specializing in local transactions, having a comparative cost advantage here, for example in its relations to certain customers and to the local or national government. This is probably more common in LICs than it is in developed countries, due to the large institutional differences between them.

Transactional disadvantages are particularly great during the initial operations of a company in a far-off LIC, the costs of information, enforcement and bargaining being high during this period. To reduce such costs, companies need to select some form of entry into the market, for example through an agent or a distributor. This reduces risks but limits opportunities for profit as well. Information costs are high due to the reliance an another party for market-specific information. Bargaining and enforcement costs may also be high because of having limited control of the marketing process. In addition, there is a value loss due to moral hazard, at the same time that transaction-specific investment is low. At this stage, the frequency of transacting (market volume) is too low to justify an investment in specialist structures. Such low commitment of resources results in low switching costs, which reduces the hold-up part of the enforcement costs. A high-control mode is traded, therefore, for a low-control mode having high flexibility (Anderson and Gatignon, 1986). Later through an increase in market volume and the accompanying commitment to a high-control mode, involving for example a subsidiary, risk is reduced. It is first at this stage that it is possible to substitute one institutional form for another in the manner implied by internalization theory. The market now has sufficient volume so that the firm can recoup the overhead which the high-control entry mode called for. If a market is large enough for the entrant to break even on the fixed costs of a high-control mode, such a substitution can likewise be made. For LICs, such a condition is often not fulfilled, particularly at early phases of industrialization.

ADAPTATIONS BETWEEN ENTRY STRATEGY AND GROUP STRUCTURE

The extension into Eastern Asia of the internationalization process of the TNCs that were studied can largely be seen as expressive of the way in which they were organized at the time. *Pacmat* had a highly decentralized geographic organization throughout the period, whereas *Conmine*'s and *Food equipment*'s organizations were originally quite decentralized, the relation of the European head office to the Asian subsidiaries being reminiscent of the mother-daughter organization type. However, since the mid-1980s, *Food equipment* had gradually divisionalized, and at the same time partly centralized, the global organization structure. Also *Conmine*, since the beginning of the 1990s, had increasingly moved away from the old mother-daughter organization and progressively integrated their Asian subsidiaries with its global product organization. This change of global organization structure also seems to have made later phases of the internationalization process more planned.

But still the emergent strategies evident in the operations of most of the TNCs in SEA differed from the more clearly planned strategies of the companies in their European and North American markets. As will be considered in greater detail later in the book, the multi-product local subsidiaries of the companies in the small markets of SEA were, and are today, more loosely connected with the group to which they belong and are controlled differently than are single-product subsidiaries operating within the main markets. Very recently the Asian subsidiaries of two of the groups (*Indcomp* and *Trans*) have become fully-fledged members of the global product organization involved. This took place in the post-establishment phase when the TNCs had grown considerably within the area and had been established there for some time. For *Trans* there is even influence in the opposite direction, such that what the organization first tried out in Eastern Asia was later implemented for the whole group.

Thus, the development of a global organizational structure for the TNCs in question occurred at the same time as strategies gradually evolved for their subsidiaries in Eastern Asia. The transition from largely emergent to more planned strategies went hand-in-hand with an increasing internationalization of company structure and the transformation of this structure in terms of a shift in the pattern of global competition from that of favouring a mother-daughter organization to a more global product organization, and in one case (*Telecom*) to a multidimensional organization. Most of the process of becoming established in the area took place when the TNCs had an organizational structure that permitted market companies considerable freedom of action in developing strategies of their own. In some cases such an organizational form for Southeast Asian subsidiaries has also remained, at the same time that it has changed considerably on the other main world markets. Strategies have become more planned as the globalization process has accelerated. This has tended to highlight the regional concept and to speed up the direct establishment process. Some TNCs, such as *Food equipment*, have later – in the post-establishment phase – reached an apparent finalization of their global product organization, resulting in increased control of their subsidiaries, top management having charge of basic strategy but leaving the specific content of strategy for the market companies to decide. Also, some TNCs such as *Homeprod, Pacmat* and *Pills*, have not changed their basic organizational set-up, maintaining a kind of umbrella strategy in which the management of the group sets general guidelines for behaviour and allows the market companies to act within these boundaries.

Despite the changes just referred to, the market companies of the TNCs in the region still appear to have considerable freedom of action. The transnational organizations, to be sure, are still largely based on the companies' business operations in the industrialized countries of Europe and North America. However, the Asian subsidiaries of the companies are only integrated into this framework in a rather loose way. There seem to be two reasons for this. First, the peripheral markets of SEA, far off geographically and culturally different as they are from the European and North American subsidiaries, are still of only marginal importance to the TNCs and are not large enough for there to be a strong interest in integrating them closely with the European parts of the organization. Second, responsiveness to local conditions is particularly important in such markets, making it undesirable to control these subsidiaries in the same way as the European subsidiaries. However, business in such markets is increasing in its importance to the companies rapidly. The more this occurs, the more important it may also appear to be to integrate the operations of these subsidiaries with those of the product companies. This has already happened for four of the TNCs and is taking place to a considerable degree for some of the others as well. This suggests a sort of three-dimensional organizational form based on the equal importance of local interests, global product interests and group management interests. Strategies will probably also become more differentiated within such organizations, with the distinction being made explicit and maintained between the planned strategies in one part of the organization and the more emergent and locally responsive strategies in others.

With such an organizational form, gradual internationalization processes for TNCs can still occur in markets such as those in SEA, particularly for such TNCs as those considered here, which are operating in high-tech industries, where differences in technological level are especially large between TNCs acting here in the role of sellers and the customer firms from less industrialized countries which are buying their products.

Internationalization in the region can be described as a process of emerging strategies that lead a company to develop an organizational structure appropriate both to these strategies and to the market structure. This process does not appear to achieve any permanent equilibrium, due to rapid developments and continual change in the international environment. Thus, evolving strategies and organizational structure must adapt to one another again and again. A given organizational form may rapidly become obsolete. Such changes can take place at a differing pace in different parts of the organization. In some geographical areas it may be quite inefficient to attempt to adapt strategy to structure in a European way, since the structures developed for Western European firms may be unfit for operations in Asia. Such a differentiation of controls is consistent with recent views concerning how coordinating mechanisms function (Martinez and Jarillo, 1989). The direct and formal tools employed earlier are in the process of being supplemented and replaced by new and more subtle coordination mechanisms that are more indirect and informal. A process such as just described is also in line with research showing a decline in the importance of formal organization as a means of controlling of strategy, in favour of internal management processes (Bartlett and Ghoshal, 1989; Ghoshal and Bartlett, 1990).

ORGANIZATION OF LOCAL TRANSACTIONS

As evident above, marketing is the major activity within SEA of the European TNCs that were studied. This makes it important that marketing strategies and how these have been adapted to local circumstances be examined. Jansson (1993) has shown that the ability of a company to compete in SEA is strongly influenced by how its marketing activities are organized. Most of the TNCs had set up their own subsidiaries, namely their marketing had been internalized. The high-technology profile of these companies, with their competitive strategies of having direct access to customers and establishing close relationships with them, demanded technically qualified salesmen and technical experts who were based in the region, something which can most effectively be organized internally. Since the break-even level is higher in internal organization than in external, it is essential that a company operating here has a broad product programme. This is quite evident in the results that were obtained highlighting differences between these companies and some of their major competitors in SEA. In establishing an internal organization, it was adjudged highly important by these TNCs that they build up a market platform to generate a profitable and sustainable business. Through being organized in this way, TNCs commit themselves to, and invest strongly in, the host country. In this way, competitive strength for selling advanced products is built up, although at the same time as the potential for setting low prices is reduced. The competitors, through their more flexible external organization, tend to have an opposite profile, this allowing them to compete for price particularly well.

A somewhat similar difference was also found between some of these European TNCs that were studied and their Japanese competitors, which could often compete well price-wise but where the European TNCs tended to be considered superior by their major customers in terms of the transfer of technology. The global organization of the TNCs also provided a competitive advantage, particularly in the marketing of projects. The major competitive strategy of the TNCs is to defend their high prices by emphasizing quality and other related variables, such as after-sales service. This is mainly done in direct marketing through their establishing and maintaining good customer relationships.

In the present section, the marketing carried on by these TNCs is illuminated by analysing their market investments from a transaction cost perspective. This is also done for the other major external transactions: those with the supplier, as well as governmental transactions.

Bilateral and Trilateral Governance

When investments in transactions are highly specific or are semi-specific, the transactions tend to be characterized by either bilateral or trilateral governance (Williamson, 1979, 1985). The major features of these external governance forms are summarized in Figure 4.4, their being compared with those of market governance. Parties that act within the framework of bilateral or trilateral governance gradually adapt to each other. Their mutual dependence increases, reducing the likelihood of their finding alternative parties within the market. Individual and organizational trust develops, mitigating against opportunistic inclinations (Jansson, 1993, chapter 2). This is a very dominant aspect of bilateral governance and a major reason for it having such a low degree of formalization of linkages. The transactions that are recurrent are regulated there by praxis. The more occasional transactions of trilateral governance are determined to a large degree by formalized rules established through agreement. In market governance, in turn, price is the main regulator, internal transactions being regulated through authority. Bilateral governance,

Figure 4.4 Main characteristics of the external governance forms

	Market governance	**Trilateral governance**	**Bilateral governance**
Main type of information carrier	Price	Rules	Praxis
Extent of bargaining	Low	High	Moderate
Main type of enforcement (controls)	Formal	Formal/informal	Informal/formal
Main type of transaction	Discrete	Occasional	Repetitive
Main type of 'contract'	Rules	Agreement	Relation
Main type of trust	Organizational	Organizational/ professional	Individual/ organizational
Importance trust	Unimportant	Important	Very important
No. of parties	Many	Very few	Few

in contrast, is characterized by informal sanctions (controls) that are both stable and flexible. Such 'flexible rigidities' survive in part through different types of safeguards, for example through mutual investments in resources and through expectations of repetitive business serving to restrain the parties from seeking advantages in the short run (reputation effects). Trust is particularly important in bilateral governance, its constraining behaviour and reducing enforcement and bargaining costs, compensating for hierarchic or market control, and reducing opportunism. Trust also reduces the costs of search and thus of information. On the other hand, the costs of establishing both individual and organizational trust are high since it takes place through repeated face-to-face contacts in which considerable time is needed for people to get to know one another, particularly when there are cross-cultural differences involved, as there are in SEA. Such non-salvageable fixed costs tend to be distributed over extended periods of time in the long-lasting relationships which characterise bilateral governance.[2,3] Trust is likewise important in trilateral governance, particularly in the establishing of linkages. However, the main safeguard in this governance form is the reaching of agreements, which opens the door to third-party arbitration. The main difference between these two closely related governance forms, bilateral and trilateral, lies in the type of safeguards they involve. Whereas in trilateral governance the linkage that is present is established by an outside party or institution, in bilateral governance the parties to a linkage are left more to themselves (Jansson, 1993, chapter 2).

Transaction-Specific Investments in SEA

The governance form found most dominant in the study is that of bilateral contracting between industrial sellers and buyers. This governance form is characterized by recurrent transactions of intermediate products that have a limited number of alternative uses or substitutes and where transaction-specific investments are low to medium in size. Trilateral governance, in contrast, is characterized by more occasional transactions involving an even more limited number of alternative applications. Switching costs are higher in this governance form. For both bilateral and trilateral governance as they are found in SEA, uncertainty tends to be medium to high.

Customer transactions

The categorization of marketing investments in SEA according to the customer and product dimensions yields four main types of case as shown in Figure 4.5.

Figure 4.5 Four main types of market investments

	DEGREE OF PRODUCT ADAPTATION TO INDIVIDUAL CUSTOMER NEEDS	
NUMBER OF CUSTOMERS	**Special products (adapted to individual customer needs)**	**Standard products (not adapted to individual customer needs)**
Few customers	High dedication *Highly specific assets*	Intermediate dedication *Semi-specific assets*
Many customers	Intermediate dedication *Semi-specific assets*	Low dedication *Non-specific assets*

Transaction-specific investment in dedicated assets can be classified as being of a low, intermediate, or high level, as illustrated in the four typical cases shown in Figure 4.5. When assets are bound or dedicated to only a few customers, the dedication of assets is high. When the number of customers increases, the assets invested in marketing become less specialized, dedication becoming anywhere from intermediate to low. As a result, companies selling special products to only a few customers tend to tie their resources both to certain specific products and certain select customers, and to therefore be classified as having highly specific assets, assets which are more expensive to redeploy than semi-specific assets are for which the company is only bound by either the customer or the product dimension. Non-specific or non-dedicated assets are more flexible and more redeployable. The classification as just described can be said to result in three main levels of switching costs, those being highest for highly specific assets, lowest for non-specific assets, and intermediate for semi-specific assets.

The TNCs studied in SEA often invest resources in customers through transferring technology to them, thereby upgrading their capacity and increasing their ability to buy advanced industrial products. An alternative for a TNC is to invest in product development aimed at the local market. Such customer or product adaptation is common to the various Southeast Asian markets. It results in highly specific and semi-specific assets, as well as non-specific assets, being strongly locked to a particular market. This third dimension, that of tie-up, makes it particularly expensive to redeploy resources invested in a specific market.

A major factor behind the internalization of sales in SEA is the matter of the high transaction costs involved in controlling the transfer of technology. This is a problem both of transfer and of appropriability, the latter problem being particularly great in SEA. Transfer to domestic customers is complicated for technologically advanced products, especially where there is both information impactedness and social impactedness and where the danger of opportunism is considerable. As Jansson (1993) has shown, transfer can take place most efficiently within the framework of bilateral or trilateral governance, since the information is tacit and is very difficult to transfer without close personal contacts, the transfer of it involving teaching, demonstration and participation.[4] This is based on human asset specificity, which adds another specificity dimension to the highly specific, semi-specific, or non-specific assets shown in Figure 4.5. The impact of various non-economic institutions, such as those of a cultural, technological or legal character also can result in transactional disadvantages, increasing problems of recognition, team organization and disclosure.[5] In addition, the fruits of the transactions may be hard to maintain rights to. Many Asian countries, for example, are known for having weak legal enforcement of rights over intellectual property. Certain cultural traits of the major business group in the area, the Chinese, reinforce this, for example their strong entrepreneurial spirit, which increases the risk that an employee, after learning as much as possible about a particular industry, will end his employment to start up his own business in competition with the TNC.

The transaction costs created by such factors can be reduced by arranging transfers through bilateral or trilateral governance. It is also vital for a TNC that it limit transaction costs through internalizing the marketing of the products and other exchanges involved in such transfers.

Maintaining arm's-length contacts with agents or distributors here has two major disadvantages compared with the internalization of transactions, namely that the transfer of technology is less efficient and appropriability gains are lower, which tends to reduce a company's performance and make it less competitive.

Supplier transactions

Assets invested in suppliers further tie a TNC to a specific country. Different types of relationships with suppliers are developed, depending on the products bought. The supplier relationships of the production units studied in SEA can be divided into two categories, depending upon the degree of linkage specificity of the investment. In the one group, relationships tend to be characterized by an intermediate degree of bonding and by switching costs of intermediate size, largely because of the development of a network of local suppliers through such relationships. Investments in non-durable, semi-specific assets are typical for such arm's-length transactions. These supplier linkages, chiefly characterized by bilateral governance, are inefficient to manage over extended geographical distances. The seller thus attempts to locate key purchasing activities as close as possible to suppliers, investing in local assets of a semi-specific kind. The other category of supplier relationships is characterized by standardized buyer-seller linkages that have a low degree of specificity. Switching costs are low because of the investment in non-specific assets. Such transactions come closer to market governance. Purchasing can be located outside the region or can take place indirectly, through different types of intermediaries.

Government transactions

Resources may also be invested in relations with the political or the governmental system, for example as represented by political parties, governments or administrative organizations, with the aim of legitimizing the business, or obtaining production or import licences, or work permits. Transaction-specific investments are also made with parties of this sort, further establishing major ties with the country. It was found that this kind of bonding varies a lot between different countries and different industries. Singapore, for example, regulates its industries much less than other ASEAN countries do. In Malaysia and Thailand, certain industries are regulated more strongly than others, companies within the regulated industries tending to have more extensive government contacts. Informational and social impactedness are usually high in such relationships.

Once established, investments of the kind just discussed reduce the negotiating power of a TNC with the government as compared with the period before the investment was made.[6] Having the TNC as a hostage, the government can press it for concessions. The power the TNC wields under such circumstances is a function of how dependent the government is on the specific assets which the company can transfer. By transferring a new and specific technology when earlier technology has become generally known and obsolete, bargaining power can be maintained. A more balanced situation can also occur if the government invests in assets which are tied to the TNC, for example in infrastructure. This is a safeguard for the foreign company. Another important factor relating to the bargaining power of a TNC is the political salience of its investment.[7]

ORGANIZATION OF THE VERTICAL PRODUCT CHAIN

The vertical organization of transactions in SEA was discussed briefly above in connection with the analysis of transaction-specific investments. Although the issue of vertical organization is of interest in itself, it also serves as an important background to the types of organization analysed in the next two chapters. In this section the question of whether a TNC has internalized or externalized different stages in the production of a product after its having established an initial sales position in a vertical product chain is discussed. The various 'make or buy' issues along the vertical product chain or the value-added chain can be seen as involving four major questions:

1. Have the sales in SEA been internalized? It was observed above that most of the European TNCs that were studied had internalized the initial stage in the local vertical product-chain – that of sales – by establishing sales subsidiaries of their own. The final products were sold by the company on the spot through a sales unit of its own rather than their being imported by the customer through an outside distributor/agent.
2. Are the products manufactured by the TNC in SEA or are they imported into the region?
3. What products and in what amounts are the products manufactured by the TNC locally at the various stages of production (vertical manufacture)?
4. Are products that are not manufactured in a company's own factory bought from local sources or are they imported? This question concerns whether production is limited to the country where the products are sold, or is carried out in a nearby country. The basic options are import, usually from a factory in Europe that belongs to the TNC, or local manufacture.

Local production means a further tie to a specific market through transaction-specific investments in physical or human assets (Williamson, 1985, p. 95). Production in a local factory owned by the TNC results in stronger ties with the country, therefore, than importing final products or sub-contracting the items. The vertical product chain can be divided into six separate stages of value-added production, starting with the raw materials and ending with the finished product. The final manufacturing stage is termed assembly. This is the seventh stage of production, the first stage being the processing of raw materials. Different intermediary products may be produced along this chain. The raw materials obtained initially (stage 1) yield processed materials (stage 2). This is followed by castings and forgings (stage 3), components and sub-assemblies (stage 4), minor and major equipment (capital goods – stage 5), and maintenance, repair and operation (MRO) items (stage 6). This results in the final products or consumer goods which are the end product of a vertical chain which uses the input products of successive various stages that utilize different kinds of equipment.

'Make or buy' problems along the value-added chain can thus be analysed in a stepwise manner. Whether a product should be produced 'in-house' or should be bought from another manufacturer is a classical problem in transaction cost analysis.[8] The main question analysed in this section is whether the whole or only a part of the transaction chain in the production of a product should be located within the country in question. The strategic issues involved all concern the question of how large a part of the transaction chain should be located in the country having the market. These can be analysed in terms of different make or buy options, as illustrated in Figure 4.3. The options involved are ones deduced from transaction-cost theory. They specify the major types of products manufactured and purchased. As seen in Figure 4.3, products already produced by the group somewhere else are mainly manufactured within SEA, whereas input products to this local production are largely imported from some internal supplier within the group. Thus, importing end-products from the group has been replaced by importing intermediary products from them. These are supplemented by other intermediary products that are obtained from outside sources and have never been manufactured by the group.[9]

An unexpected finding of the study is that so few components are subcontracted to the region from the European factories, which means that the category 'products previously produced by the group' found in Figure 4.3 is uncommon. Thus, the TNCs that were studied largely failed to take advantage of the lower costs involved, despite the fact that some of them had marked opportunities for doing so. One reason for this is that powerful labour unions in the home countries are against this. In any case, international subcontracting of this sort is common in the area, many TNCs, although not those studied here, reducing manufacturing costs by taking advantage of the lower labour costs in the free-trade zones.

Vertical Product Structures

The manufacturing carried out regionally varies with the production and transaction costs. Examples of factors that influence costs of the latter type are those of trade secrets impacted into the production process, the existence of an adequate supplier structure, uncertainty in buying from local suppliers, and the costs of moral hazard. Different types of relationships are developed with suppliers depending on the products bought. As shown above the governance of supplier transactions is chiefly bilateral, as most customer relationships are, something which is inefficient to manage over extended geographical distances. Key purchasing activities tend, therefore, to be located closer to suppliers.

The vertical integration, or hierarchical organization, of the vertical product structures of five of the TNCs that carry out manufacturing within SEA is the same as found in European manufacturing. The entire production process is rather simple and quite possible to transfer. As Jansson (1982, 1984) has shown, it is likely that a production investment in a remote area by a TNC will result in a vertical structure similar to the one prevailing at the TNC's main production base, normally the home country. The company then produces the same products of the same quality in both locations. The vertical product structures of four other TNCs are integrated into SEA to a lesser degree than in the case of the five TNCs discussed above. For the four, assembly is carried out in SEA, whereas the components are manufactured by the group at its European location and are then imported. Since the minimum optimal scales of production for these components are large, it is not economical to have them produced locally, either 'in-house' or by external suppliers.

External factors that had a major impact on the vertical product structure of the TNCs in SEA included the structure of the local supplier markets and the actions and industrial policies of the local governments. Infrastructure did not create any major problems for the TNCs in the countries where they operated and during the period in which they were studied.

Supplier market structure

Local suppliers fail to exist for many of the products. Even when they do exist, their technical capacity is often too low and their prices too high. Generally speaking, the possibilities in the area for purchasing locally are still poor due to the relatively low degree of industrialization. Singapore is an exception. However, this is a small country in which there is little room in most industries for any particular depth of industrial structure such that there are several different stages of value-added processing. Thus, technological and external factors contribute to the situation of the manufacturing subsidiaries of TNCs purchasing few input products that are made locally. Such a state of affairs was found in the study to be strengthened by the policy of not externalizing products that are manufactured by the TNC. Thus, most TNCs did not attempt to adapt to conditions or to change them but continued to import input products into the area. The small to medium-sized companies within SEA lacked the resources to be able to influence their environment to any appreciable extent. Despite the demand for technological inputs, their resources were not sufficient to enable them to integrate backwards into areas in which they had no previous expertise and in which their production technologies were unrelated to the production technologies of the inputs that were required. If local suppliers could not be found for technological products, such products had to be imported.

Government policy

For two of the TNCs (*Trans* and *Telecom*) it was found that the production subsidiaries in a country had been forced by the government there to indigenize their buying. This had not stopped them from purchasing products manufactured internally by the group, however. The production units had simply switched from foreign external suppliers to local external suppliers. The government was part of the process of developing local suppliers in both a direct and an indirect way, working actively for establishing linkages between buyers and suppliers and establishing rules for limiting foreign imports, with the aim of spurring industrial development. The policy thus exemplified represents a basic framework for the industrial development of a country, since it determines in what order and at what pace various supplier industries are developed and thus the possibilities for indigenous procurement. A lack of industrial development makes indigenous purchases impossible or delays supplier development. The means used to implement policies varies between countries and also between different industries within a given country. All ASEAN countries except Singapore have a trade regime that exerts an influence upon purchasing possibilities, for example through the levying of tariffs. Some of the measures are aimed at TNCs directly, for example stipulations regarding the buying of equipment from local producers. In some of the countries and for some of the industries studied, a combination of direct and indirect measures, such as a combination of tariffs and duties, was employed. Measures were taken, therefore, to further the development of local suppliers and to protect them from international competition.

The government has an important impact, therefore, on transaction costs, particularly during the establishment of local suppliers, or infant industrial period. There is substantial inertia here for a TNC to overcome, an inertia that has a negative effect both on the TNC and also in an indirect way on the government, an inertia resulting in high transaction costs. For example, on the one hand, TNCs are expected or required to indigenize as much of their production as possible; on the other hand, they may be forced in this way to include in the production process expensive stages which could make local production uncompetitive on world markets.

The overall needs and production structures of SEA subsidiaries seemed to make it difficult for them to adapt to local conditions. Their chances for externalizing technology products were limited. An important factor in their not purchasing technology products from local suppliers seems to have been the high transaction costs involved, due to the uncertainty present and the opportunism that occurred, as well as the costs due to economies of scale (large differences in indivisibilities).

A general observation gained from the study was that the situation found on the local supplier market was similar to that with which TNCs were faced within the customer markets. The level of technical capability was low generally and its variation large, it being highest among suppliers affiliated with TNCs and lowest for the local Chinese firms. The suppliers affiliated with TNCs are larger, are organized differently and have better chances of succeeding than is the case for the local companies, which are more concerned with price than with quality and are more short-sighted in their behaviour than the larger firms.

PRODUCTION COSTS AND TRANSACTION COSTS

As observed in Chapter 2 and confirmed in this study, the decision to establish a sales company concerns the establishing of a hierarchical firm. The establishing of a production unit in such far-off markets, on the other hand, is more of a multi-plant investment decision, since production costs are the major issue. In this book, manufacturing is viewed from an organizational economics perspective, where different stages of production are located in relation to the customer being determined by information costs, bargaining costs and enforcement costs. This accords with transaction costs being conceived as the major marketing costs required for bridging and organizing the gaps between sellers and buyers (Jansson, 1993). Costs for the transfer of solutions are included here, but not the production costs for the manufacturing of a product. Certain costs closely connected with manufacturing are treated as transaction costs and not as production costs, for example those inventory costs and transport costs that represent the costs of transferring a solution.

Manufacturing costs are thus concerned here as the costs for producing an item, specifically the costs of the factory and the costs for the production carried out there. Production costs and transaction costs are related in various ways. For example, even if transaction costs might be lowered by moving production closer to customers, high manufacturing costs due to not being able to take advantage of economies of scale may inhibit this. The question was thus examined here of how transaction costs are constrained by various aspects of the companies' manufacturing, for example their economies of scale and their production technology. A connection in the other direction, one should note, also exists, for example transaction frequency (market size) and the degree of transaction-specific investment affecting the costs of transport, of tariffs and of multiplant economies (Nicholas, 1986, p. 74). Transaction costs and production costs, as well as the relation between the two, are also influenced by other institutional factors. A production investment could, for example, be based on onmarket factors such as government stipulations. As Williamson (1985, pp. 90-5) has shown, the relative importance of production costs and transaction costs varies with the degree of asset specificity. Market procurement rather than own production is most favourable when there are economies of scale in production and when asset specificity is low:

> The production cost penalty of using internal organization is large for standardized transactions for which market aggregation economies are great. (Ibid., p. 92)

Added to this are various governance costs, e.g. bureaucratization costs. Internal organization is advantageous when the opposite conditions predominate.

> Not only does the market realize little aggregate economy benefits, but market governance, because of the 'lock-in' problems that arise when assets are highly specific, is hazardous. (Ibid., p. 94)

In mixed cases, between these two extremes, there are no definite answers of this sort. Size is important, since large firms tend more than small to be organized in terms of component parts. The possibility here of aggregating transactions internally so as to take advantage of both economies of scale and scope is considered as important in this book, a major question dealt with being the comparative economics for TNCs of spreading their production out geographically so as to locate it in various countries versus centralizing it to only a few specific locations.

It can thus be concluded that both transaction costs and production costs influence vertical product structures. For example, the high production efficiencies achieved through economies of scale in many industries tend to create oligopolistic market structures, which may increase between-firm bargaining costs. On the other hand, the high uncertainty often experienced by TNCs operating in developing countries may lead them to take up the 'in-house' production of certain inputs, in which case low internal demand may result in low production efficiency owing to the insufficient use of economies of scale.

It is hard to change a TNC's vertical product structure or the transaction cost and production cost structure of the internal and external manufacturing involved in its operations in various countries. High technological dependence, as for example in the assembly and production of components, increases the readiness to integrate. It also leads to recurrent transactions, which are more easily internalized than occasional or one-time transactions are. At the same time, internalization of technology products implies high transaction costs for a company of learning the ins and outs of new technology. There may also be additional production costs due to the need for investing in new machines. Such expenses are lacking, for the most part, when capacity products are internalized. Markets for technology products can thus be internalized through vertical integration, the costs for switching to internal production needing to be counter-balanced by lowering transaction costs or production costs so as to motivate such a move. Vertical disintegration may also take place when 'in house' production is too expensive, for example where internal demand is too low to achieve economies of scale or where uncertainty is too high, for example regarding future demand or the access to labour and other inputs. Institutional deficiences may result here in information, bargaining and enforcement costs for internal production being too high, making production and transaction costs lower through the market. Also, special technology products are more likely to be internalized than are standard technology products, since their switching costs are lower because of linkage-specific investments already having been made.

The internal structure of the production subsidiary, involving its vertical product structure, size, and production technology, and group structure, affects its vertical integration. The relatively small size of the markets in SEA affects both the possibilities of achieving economies of scale in a company's own factories there and in suppliers' factories due to the low demand for inputs. The situation can be summarized as follows: the degree of vertical integration achieved for standard technology products is mainly decided by differences in production costs, whereas both production costs and transaction costs are relevant to the vertical integration achieved for special technology products.

CONCLUSIONS

Traditional studies of the internationalization process can be seen as too narrow, since they fail to take account of how such activities are organized. A broader framework was utilized here, internationalization being analysed in terms of strategies and of multinational organizational structures, as well as from a transaction cost perspective.

The pattern found for the establishment of TNCs within this geographical area seems similar to the establishment pattern described by Johanson and Wiedersheim-Paul (1975) in their learning process model of internationalization. It involves an incremental cumulative learning process in which commitment increases with improved knowledge of the geographical area. The sort of establishment chain reported earlier seems valid.

There were certain deviations from this overall or average pattern and thus from the model referred to above. The establishment of some market companies was more direct and took place without an agent of the company having been found in the market previously. This was particularly the case late in the regional establishment phase when an improved knowledge of the geographical area by the TNCs coincided with rapid economic growth in most of the markets of the region. This does not contradict the basic model, particularly if the establishment process is viewed from a regional perspective rather than from the perspective of an individual country.

In countries in which foreign firms were not allowed to operate sales companies or manufacturing companies, no internationalization process of the sort described in the model was found. A TNC was represented simply by agents or distributors. Agents were also found, in some cases in which TNCs were allowed to have sales companies, to be retained by a TNC alongside the sales companies, the two existing parallel to each other.

A crucial connection was found between a TNC's entry strategy and its global organization structure, their affecting each other mutually and in turn being affected by the market structure. One direction of effects involves the market structure affecting the TNC's strategy, and this in turn affecting its organizational structure. However, for an establishment strategy in a specific geographical area the direction of effects could be reversed. A given global organization structure can affect how a TNC established itself in a local market, which in turn can result in a specific market structure. This can result, for example, in a kind of replica of the world market developing in a local market.

An external organization form was found to be efficient in the early stages of a TNC's involvement in Southeast Asian markets, especially through its reducing the risks inherent in an uncertain environment. Flexibility, or low switching costs, was seen as a key aspect of this type of organization, which requires little investment in specialist structures, and facilitates the change of agents often required in the region due to its rapidly shifting business conditions. Indeed, the frequency of transactions is usually too low at the initial stages to justify an investment in specialist structures. Eventually the market volume grows to a level that justifies investment in a sales company. In some countries, however, TNCs keep their agents either because internal sales organizations are not allowed or because internal organization is only efficient for certain transactions.

Marketing investments were found to mainly be of a transaction-specific kind in which resources were bound either to highly specific or to semi-specific assets. Transactions with industrial products were of either the recurrent or the occasional type and to involve either high or intermediate uncertainty. TNCs often invested resources in customer relations through transferring technology to them and upgrading their capacity. This is both a transfer and an appropriability problem. The transfer to domestic customers of specific technologically superior assets characterized by information impactedness and opportunism tends to be complicated. The tacit knowledge involved is very difficult to transfer without close personal contacts.

Although supplier transactions are usually characterized by bilateral governance as well, the degree of asset-specificity is lower. On the whole, both customer and supplier transactions, distinguished as they are by bilateral governance, are inefficient to manage over long geographical distances. Sellers thus tend to locate their key marketing and purchasing activities closer to buyers and suppliers, internalizing these activities within the TNC organization. The degree to which further ties to the country in question were sought by investing in government relationships was found to vary a great deal between the TNCs that were studied.

A decision to establish a hierarchy was taken together with the sales company, whereas a decision regarding establishment of a production unit was a multi-plant investment decision that was largely based on earlier market investments. Few of the products sold by the TNCs studied here were manufactured within SEA. And local manufacturing of these products which occurred tended to be carried out in small plants, the purchasing locally of materials and components for production there also playing only a minor role. When products were manufactured within SEA, those components produced by the group were imported. A complementary buying of products manufactured locally that had never been produced by the group took place too. Such a pattern of favouring internal transactions is in accordance with the transaction cost perspective adopted in this book.

The strategic purchasing option open to the TNCs studied here was to either import a product that was required or buy it from local suppliers. The make or buy alternatives for capacity products was not available for these companies within SEA. For five of the TNCs, the hierarchical organization of vertical product structures was the same as for manufacturing in Europe. The manufacturing of four of the others was not closely integrated with operations in SEA, since little more than the assembly of parts was carried out there. The various patterns present can be explained in terms of a transaction cost and production cost analysis of vertical product structures involved which in turn are influenced by group structure and policy as well as by external structure. The narrowing of even non-existent supplier markets in SEA was a major deterrent to the possibility of indigenizing purchasing. Also, government policy affected the purchasing strategies of the TNCs in several of the countries and of the different industries. The high transaction costs involved in developing local supplier sources could be reduced by building up and maintaining good buyer/seller relationships. To a large part these problems on the supplier side were similar to those analysed on the customer side, for example the low levels of technical capability, the importance of contact nets, and the predisposition of the Chinese firms to price competition.

NOTES

1. Technology products are products that, in the short run, at least, the buyer cannot produce with the production equipment and knowledge at hand, and which are therefore purchased. Capacity products, on the other hand, are ones produced both by the buyer and the seller.
2. Compare Hennart (1982, pp. 97-104).
3. This can also be illustrated by the basic contracting schema, developed by Williamson (1985). Relations involving asset-specificities are balanced if there are safeguards. If such safeguards are missing, the relationship becomes unstable. If trust is low, this increases transaction costs due to the haggling which occurs or the higher risk for the breakdown of the relationship. The break-even supply price is higher here, the seller compensating for the higher risk by raising the price.
4. See also Williamson, 1985 and Teece, 1981.
5. An example is that of their high entrepreneurial spirit, which increases the risk that an employee after learning about an industry, ends his employment to start his own business and compete with the TNC (Jansson, 1987).
6. For a further discussion of this aspect, see Teece (1986, pp. 38-43), Mahini and Wells (1986), and Casson (1987, p. 135).
7. This type of analysis of government-TNC relationships is taken up in detail by Behrman and Grosse (1990). For an analysis of the political behaviour of TNCs as network strategies in dealings with government, see Jansson and Sharma (1993), Jansson, Sharma and Saqib (1993).
8. See, for example, Andersson and Weitz (1983), Butler and Carney (1983), Jansson (1982), Monteverde and Teece (1982), Walker and Weber (1984), Williamson (1985).
9. These results provide strong support for theories of the TNC based on transaction cost, for example internalization theory and the eclectic paradigm.

5. Local Organization within the Global Product Organization

Competition between, and satisfaction of, three main types of interests that have been referred to – company-wide interests, product group interests, and local interests – is a main feature of the transnational M-form. In this chapter local interests are of prime concern, implying a kind of bottom-up perspective on the organization of the TNC. The basic make-up of the local organization in the TNCs that were studied was indicated earlier in Table 1.2. The importance placed on the local rationale, or the geographic dimension, in the decomposition of global structure of a TNC varies with the company, sometimes receiving emphasis, sometimes less, and sometimes about the same emphasis as the product dimension. It was observed in Chapters 3 and 4 that among the TNCs that were studied the mother-daughter type organization was more common in earlier periods than in later periods and that today many of the TNCs in question have changed to an organization based on product companies,[1] having established a global product organization and having a form of organization centred on product companies or divisions. An important reason is that often they sell high-technology products and that therefore technical and product-related matters are more central to efficiency than adaptation to local markets.[2] Such a global product type organization is by far the most common among the TNCs that were studied. For this reason, the chapter at hand is devoted entirely to the local organization here and its impact on the global product organization as a whole.

One of the main findings of the investigation of European TNCs in SEA presented here is that the organization locally is usually a compromise between existing group structure and local conditions, and that organization at the local level also affects the global product organization. The global structure tends to be segmented along the vertical dimension, a trade-off being made between global product interests and local market interests, implying the horizontal coordination between the vertical segments to be only slight. The efficiency of the global product organization is therefore determined by how effectively a mechanism for a translation of local demands into 'supplies' to be obtained from the group is established and maintained. The smaller a subsidiary is, the more unbalanced the vertical relationship here and the more difficult it is to achieve efficiency in such a trade-off. At the beginning of the operations in SEA, the global product organization is usually in so far as possible reproduced directly and a clear priority given to efficiency as seen from the perspective of the global product company, this amounting to a low degree of responsiveness to local conditions. This mismatch between the product company and market company makes the organization of the TNC as a whole inefficient. This can result in suboptimality of both the marketing strategy and the market organization within the local market.

Thus, if there is to be an efficient trade-off between global integration and local responsiveness within the global product organization, it is critical to develop a 'coupling mechanism' between the 'pipelines' coming from the product companies and the 'pipelines' coming from the markets. This principle is shown in Figure 5.1. The experience of one of *Tooltec*'s market companies illustrates this trade-off quite well. The subsidiary in question has gradually changed its organization from that of a product-company (straight pipelines) orientation with a sales organization largely directed at the maintenance of European standards, to that of a company more strongly oriented to the local market. The front organization, or sales, is now organized according to the type of needs involved (of the customer and of industry), the old organization having only been kept in its purchasing function.

Figure 5.1 Global product/local market activity grid

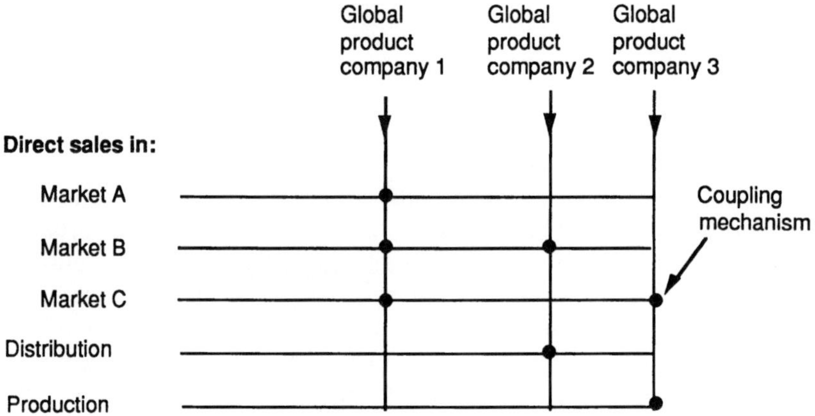

Since all the products sold are bought from the group, it is essential that the group's product company organization be reflected on the input side. Critical local organizational issues are expressed through this grid or mechanism of translation between the local customers and the product companies, using it for example to adapt a budget oriented to the local customers to the group's budget system, which is based on the products involved. Since the local organization adapts continually to the shifting needs of the customer, the organization has an organic character. This new market organization has also made it possible to change the incentive system of the salesmen. Whereas a traditional local-bonus system based on group performance was employed earlier, that in use now is based on individual performance. This change has made it possible to build up a feedback system that frequently informs the individual salesman regarding his or her current performance. This has increased efficiency. Salesmen now devote virtually all their time and energy to selling in the market, whereas 'purchasers' maintain the contacts with the product companies, and sales managers manage the grid.

An efficient market organization is critical for keeping up the competitive strength of the firm. The better marketing is organized, the more difficult it is for competitors to imitate. This trend toward a more market-oriented organization was found for the market companies of other TNCs as well. Transaction costs were reduced by adapting the market approach to the products and increasing control of the salesmen. In the beginning, the Chinese salesmen had been largely left to themselves, it seeming to have been a common belief that, due to their high entrepreneurial spirit, they should be given a degree of freedom. In addition to the changes just mentioned, local group-oriented bonus systems were adopted. However, this adaptation of the sales organization to local conditions seems to have gone too far in some of the market companies, particularly in connection with the direct selling of technically complex industrial products. One drawback of this was that individual salesmen tended to be lacking in insight into market developments generally and were thus in need of central guidance.

MIXED AND SINGLE LOCAL ORGANIZATIONS

As shown in Chapter 3, a major characteristic of the global product organization is that it extends the vertical pipelines, or the vertical value chains, throughout the organization to all the relevant world markets. The TNCs that were studied organized the gap between the product dimension and the geographic dimension in different ways and with mixed results. When product companies need to share a sales subsidiary, special problems arise, since this tends to segregate the organization into two main parts, one involving single-division subsidiaries and the other involving multi-division subsidiaries. The former is a pure global product organization, whereas the latter either becomes an organization of pure geographic form or assumes certain characteristics similar to those of the mother-daughter (multinational) organizational form, in part on the basis of how subsidiaries are controlled by group management. The line of demarcation between such main types of organization within the same group organization becomes arbitrary, for example as regards the control of mixed subsidiaries and their role within the group. This can be illustrated here by four groups (*Conmine*, *Match*, *Drives* and *Homeprod*). The borders in these cases between the respective organizational types are oblique and fluid, largely because management does not seem to be aware of the main differences that have been created between single-division and multi-division subsidiaries. As still another case (*Tooltec*) demonstrates, one solution to these problems would be to change the mother-daughter organization into a more pure geographic organization, the product dimension and the geographic dimension being separated from each other. One result of this would be a better demarcation of the respective borders, for instance, between group management and product division management regarding the responsibility for control of the different types of subsidiaries. At the same time, certain TNCs established within the larger Asian markets but involved in only a limited number of areas of business have been able to basically reproduce their global product organization in Asia. The potential advantages of copying the group organization at the local market level as compared with maintaining a mixed organization are clearly shown by two cases (*Trans* and *Indcomp*). One solution to the growing complexity in world markets is to abandon a one-dimensional organizational form such as that of the global product organization in favour of a multidimensional type of organization. *Telecom*'s transformation into an organization of this type was examined in Chapter 3. This is taken up again at the end of the chapter.

Global Product Organization Mixed with the Mother-Daughter Organization

The problems for a complex world organization in controlling small sales subsidiaries located in remote markets were illustrated at the beginning of the book for the case of one of *Conmine's* market companies in SEA. As noted there, bad business practice and the failure to take advantage of profit potentials remained unnoticed for years, primarily because of a lack of adequate control of the subsidiary by the group. The subsidiary became too locally responsive when the group basically lost control by dismantling the regional organization.

This latter group is highly decentralized and has many characteristics in common with the multinational organizational type (the mother-daughter type of organization), especially as regards its small subsidiaries located in far-off markets. The subsidiary in question was ranked in terms of size at only position 35 or thereabouts among the 60 sales subsidiaries. An 80-20 rule is employed within the group, meaning that group management is to devote approximately 80% of its attention to some 20% of the subsidiaries. Since most of group management's control capacity is taken up by the largest subsidiaries, located in Europe and North America, the control of the smaller sales subsidiaries is only loose and the knowledge about them within the group is low. Reporting requirements for them are also lower, the standard format involved being adapted to the size of the subsidiary. The subsidiary examined here sends the same type of report to all the parties concerned. These reports are usually not followed up as long as the bottom-line figures reported are basically acceptable. As the case illustrates, such figures can easily be too crude to serve as control indicators. However, even though the reporting requirements were raised for subsidiaries of this type recently, output control for the group is still less tight than that of many of the other groups that were studied. Financial reporting now takes place every month and sales reporting every quarter. Thus, within the mother-daughter type of organization the budgetary reporting system for subsidiaries tends generally to be less extensive. This difference in reporting requirements illustrates another characteristic of the groups that were studied – the separation of ownership control from hierarchical (operational) control, only hierarchical control being considered in any detail here.

Mix of product divisions

Conmine does not seem to have had any clear policy regarding the role of its subsidiaries in SEA. Should a particular subsidiary, for example, serve as a pure sales company (an implementer) or should it also have certain regional functions such as being a supply centre or an overseer of distributors in the region? How should it be linked to the three main business areas of the group? The last issue can be illustrated by the case of a very profitable distributor that was transferred from one subsidiary to a different one. This was due to its having been shown, through complaints by the distributor after a few years of operation, that the subsidiary could not give the distributor sufficient marketing and technical support. Since this subsidiary lacked knowledge of the distributor's main field of business, the distributor was transferred to a new subsidiary which possessed such knowledge. This was a formalization of a relationship that in fact had already existed for several years on an informal basis. Consequently, for a certain period the distributor formally belonged to one subsidiary but developed considerable business informally with another.

This case illustrates a major organizational problem which the industrial groups that were studied had in the distant Asian markets: how to relate their smaller subsidiaries to the firm's business areas or product divisions, where it is only in large markets that the principle of each business area having its own sales subsidiaries can be sure to succeed. *Conmine*, for instance, has three parallel subsidiaries in Germany, each subordinated to a particular business area. The Southeast Asian subsidiary was only recently subordinated to one of the business areas or divisions and its profits consolidated there. Previous to that, it had been assigned to the group management directly, despite its business having always been carried on with this division. It is now subordinated both to the division in question and to group management. This change of organization means that the specialization or role of the subsidiary has been formalized. Since it is mainly to represent one of the firm's business areas within SEA, its relations with the other business areas of the firm have been more loosely formalized in terms of an agency relationship. As a consequence of being only an agent for these other business areas, it is not really interested in marketing these other lines of products. Thus, the TNC has problems in using this subsidiary as a sales outlet for the other lines of products. At the same time, if the subsidiary should become interested in developing in a serious way a market for some new product belonging to one of the other business areas or product lines, the management of the business area in question might not be interested. This is a real problem in Southeast Asian markets, which are too small to allow for separate subsidiaries of the European type. The choice for the various business areas of the group is thus between having an internal 'agent' or an external one. The basic question behind the issues involved concerns how 'mixed' a subsidiary should be. How should the internal competition between product divisions be organized, and how many products need to be sold for a minimum scale of operations to be achieved for the group's establishing a sales subsidiary.

Trade-off of control between group management and product division management

This problem of the linkage between business areas and subsidiaries is part of a larger organizational problem within the groups, namely how to achieve an efficient trade-off between business area management and group management in the control of individual subsidiaries. Until quite recently, *Conmine*'s subsidiaries in SEA were formally organized under group management, one of the executive vice presidents being responsible for the companies located in that part of the world. During the initial years of operation, this managerial position was based in Europe, but it is now based in the Asian-Pacific area. This is a betterment for the Asian subsidiaries and there are now more meetings per year (four) as well. Group management can maintain better control through having more adequate knowledge of the subsidiaries' operations, at the same time as local management is directed in its undertakings in a better way and now has much better possibilities for discussing its problems with the very well-informed vice president.

In the new organization, the subsidiary finds itself in a kind of two-dimensional organization, in which the manager for the country in question has two executive vice presidents above him, one representing one of the business areas and the other representing group management. A divisionalized TNC can never escape a conflict of this sort. Rather its main organizational task is simply that of reducing the conflict as much as possible. As will be analysed more for *Conmine* in Chapter 6, transfer pricing is one of the main means of control in this respect. The need of control is also shown by the fact that, while the subsidiary was still only subordinated to group management, its interest was to increase its own profit at the expense of other units. This sometimes led to not particularly honest arguments with the business area or product line regarding prices. There were instances too of cheating and lying. With the increase in the formal importance of the business area to the subsidiary, however, and the consolidation of profits within the business area instead of within the group generally, there is less reason to compete internally and more reason in pricing to consider only the external competitive situation. There is less reason to 'show off' to group management. A more differentiated profit statement makes it possible to better observe where profits originate. This increased hierarchical control of the subsidiary by linking it to only one division also results in a more united group response to outside competition and there being less internal competition. Transaction costs are reduced by increasing hierarchical control and decreasing market control.

The unclear position of the subsidiary has also meant an unclear role for the managing director of the subsidiary. Some of the incumbents have had more of a typical general management outlook with a strong orientation to group management and have been more interested in managing than in selling. This was especially true during the establishment period, when the managing director was recruited from another TNC and worked closely with four other expatriates likewise located in positions of leadership. Other managing directors have been more of the typical salesman type and have been more down-to-earth and more locally oriented. This change in company cultures has increased the uncertainty of the subsidiary further, for instance regarding its role and where it belongs within the group. In a highly decentralized group organization the job of being manager for the country becomes an extremely important position, since it unites three different roles: that of 'bicultural interpreter', of 'national defender and advocate', and of 'front-line implementer' (Bartlett and Ghoshal, 1991). As is evident the combination of these roles at the subsidiary changed over time.

There are a number of regional functions such as that of supply, that are permanently located at the sales subsidiary that is most centrally located in the region. The product experts, temporarily stationed at this subsidiary for a few years to support the various sales subsidiaries in the region, are paid for by the business areas in question and therefore only rent office space. The subsidiary in question also shares the managing director with the sales subsidiary of a neighbouring country. This is mainly made possible by the fact that both subsidiaries sell the same group products. In a way, these two subsidiaries can be looked upon as representing a region, albeit a small one. A similar thing is taking place in one of the Northeast Asian areas.

This case illustrates the problems in finding a combination of controls able to reduce the inefficiency caused by there being too little outside control of local transactions. The basic management control situation faced by *Conmine* is shown in Figure 5.2. Subsidiaries for which local responsiveness is particularly important are at an obvious risk of becoming too independent. The inefficiency of control is reflected in high information and enforcement costs due to decisions and the implementation of them being inferior. A faulty incentive structure favours opportunistic behaviour, which also increases bargaining costs, noted among other things in the pricing behaviour. All in all this results in suboptimization. Transaction costs for the group were reduced by improving the balance found, on the one hand, between the control exerted by group management (GM) against control by the global product division management (GPM) and, on the other hand, between the different product divisions. A change in organization led to a reduction in opportunism and an improvement in the long-term profits of the group.

Figure 5.2 Main conflicts of interest at Conmine

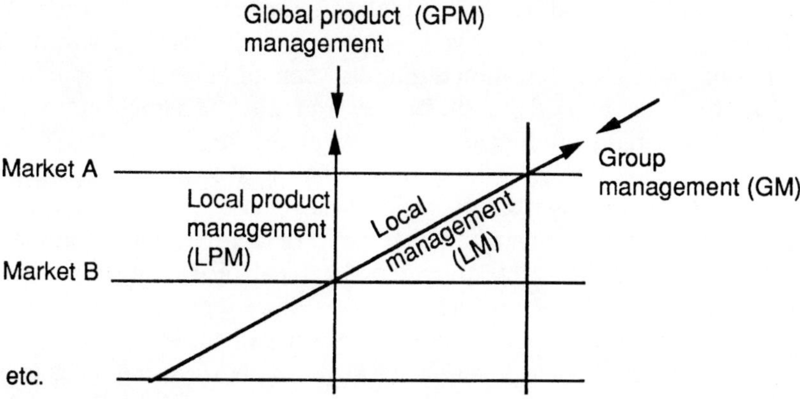

Unequal internationalization of the product groups

The problem of the linkage between the product divisions and the subsidiaries, as just discussed, found in *Conmine* can be exacerbated if the degree of internationalization varies between product companies. A major problem here concerns the possibility of using the international organization already established as a route for other products the TNC produces. Problems of a similar character may arise when a new product dissimilar to earlier products is introduced. In one of the TNCs that were studied (*Match*), one of the product companies had a much larger international market organization towards the end of the

1980s than the other product companies in the group. In addition, the differences between the product companies were large, since the group was very diversified. The market companies already established by the group were difficult for other product companies to utilize as a means of extending their internationalization. Since both the capacity and the market contacts for such new products were lacking, much support from the product company that was investing was called for. Even if an individual market company agreed to represent a new product of this sort produced within the group, resistance from other parts of the established market organization was hard, for example from the regional unit. An alternative for such an internationally rather inexperienced product company was to establish an international organization of its own. However, this was usually too expensive in the small Southeast Asian markets. As a result, some sort of compromise usually had to be reached.

A change from single-product subsidiary to multi-product subsidiary imposed by a centralized merger

The small regional sales organization of *Drives* had had two main types of internal organization during its years of being in operation in SEA. Until the end of the 1980s, the firm was the representative of one of two main product lines of one of the smaller of the TNCs studied in the project. This product line was ordinarily managed through the firm's own sales subsidiaries, something which is not the case for the other product line, that was marketed entirely to governments, and for the sales of which the local organization form is represented by a joint venture. Hence, a clear separation was made between the organization of these product lines both at the global and at the local level, each level living a life of its own, the sales subsidiary studied concentrating, therefore, on one main line of business for many years. Since the subsidiary was autonomous, the relation to the group could be characterized as that of a mother-daughter organization.

At the end of the 1980s, however, when the European parent company merged with an American TNC, the situation changed drastically. This reinforced a previously small product line of the group, which joined with the American TNC to become a new and important product division. The merger of these companies has been very problematic and has taken much time and considerable resources to implement, that part of the merger involving the two sales organizations in Asia included. The amalgamation of the TNCs was especially difficult due to a number of additional factors – that the merger took place during a recession, that the decision to merge was taken at very high levels without consultations with the lower levels, and that the technological capabilities of one of the TNCs was misjudged by the other. Whereas the American TNC had had an area-based organization earlier, one that was well-established in Asia, the European TNC had a mother-daughter type of organization. Both these organizations are now merging into a global product organization, a new product line being established in what were formerly single-line units, the subsidiaries being divided up among the two major product lines in accordance with the line tending to dominate the company's sales.

Further problems are yet to be solved. The subsidiary studied has changed to a multi-line company, which has brought on many of the problems for such a unit that were discussed above. At the beginning of the 1990s the subsidiary is still dominated by the old product line and is as independent as it was earlier. However, sales for the other product division have increased considerably in recent years. This division is now represented locally by an expert who is responsible for the sales of its products, but who reports to Hong Kong, where the regional representation for the product division, belonging to the earlier American part of the organization is located. This linkage does not seem to work particularly well yet, since the Southeast Asian representative, who comes from the smaller European part of that product division and thus has stronger ties to that part of the organization than to the American part, operates in a very independent way. The linkage to Hong Kong is also of very low formal significance, since the subsidiary as a whole is still assigned to group management headquarters and reports there, which in turn distributes the reports further to those concerned, for example to the product divisions and the Hong Kong unit. The new situation also has arbitrary aspects, for instance as regards the distribution of responsibility for profits between the different interests. Conflicts of interest are created both between the two product divisions and between these and the group. The situation in SEA is further complicated by the fact that one expatriate person represents one of the product divisions and is the managing director of the subsidiary, whereas the other expatriate person represents the other product division. This is the well-known problem, already discussed, of a mixed subsidiary that falls outside the main organization for the group. Product divisions have to share the overhead of an established subsidiary, since the small markets in SEA do not allow for the existence of separate subsidiaries in this respect. Another typical problem, analysed previously for a mixed subsidiary, concerns the major product line 'crowding out' the others. This has been solved in the company by assigning responsibility for the profits of the minor line to the product expert, who is no longer merely a coordinator and a technical expert, but is also a product manager.

The costs for employing two expatriates in a rather small subsidiary are high. However, since each of them is a technical product expert, a salesman, and a sales manager combined, and one of them is also managing director, they succeed very well on their own, do not need assistance from the home base, and take up very little of the group's control capacity. Another of the Asian subsidiaries, in contrast, has only a local administrative managing director, receives considerable technical support, support which the product divisions provide for the salesmen who were engaged locally. Such local employees in markets of a cultural character far from headquarters also tend to lack socialization into the corporate culture. The trade-offs involved are decided finally by how complicated the products sold are and what control structure best increases the group's long-term profits through producing a maximum reduction in transaction costs.

This case suggests how trade-offs can be made between input control, output control, and behaviour control so as to solve conflicts between the three major interests found within the transnational M-form: local interests, global product interests and group interests. The relationships here are shown in Figure 5.3. Although the group has

Figure 5.3 Main conflicts of interest at Drives

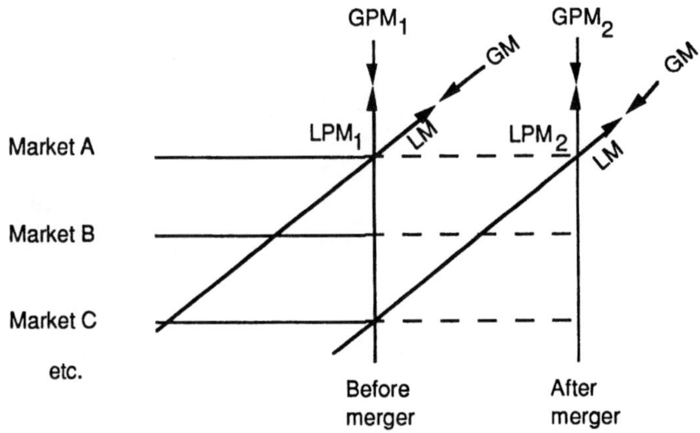

more frequent contacts with the Hong Kong office regarding one of the product lines, the total control it is able to exert over that office is less due to its own representation there being weaker. Indeed, a subsidiary that is manned by locals seems to come closer to an external form of organization than does one manned by expatriates from the group. The case also shows the high costs involved in enforcing at the local level decisions taken at the global level. Conflicts arise which increase bargaining costs and transaction costs further. These costs reduce considerably the potential gains of a merger that are believed to take place through cost savings from economies of scale and economies of scope (synergies).

The Global Product Organization Separated from the Mother-Daughter Organization

Homeprod's global organization consists of 19 product-line companies which have worldwide responsibility for their products and are grouped into five business areas. In a few cases there is a dual responsibility of European and American units for a given product line. This is well motivated from a marketing standpoint but sometimes leads to suboptimization in production. The majority of the subsidiaries represent only one product line and therefore report to the manager of one of the single-product line companies. Multi-product line companies, in contrast, represent several product-lines within a country and thus report directly to group management. These latter companies are mainly found within smaller markets, such as those in SEA. *Homeprod*'s group organization is very decentralized, which makes its organizational form very flat in structure due to the many product lines and the few hierarchical levels of command. The main issues of control for a multi-product line subsidiary within such a global organization are shown in Figure 5.4.

Local organization

Basic differences in the company culture of the group and of the subsidiaries in SEA can be noted. The latter show more long-term thinking and a more philosophical orientation. A vivid company culture should penetrate the entire organization at the same time as profits should not be seen as the one and only mission of the company. For a group to be successful in this region of the world, it is important that it take account of the inherent elements of company culture and adapt to these. This can be difficult, however, since local values may be very opposed to group values and be hard to understand at the global

Figure 5.4 Main conflicts of interest at Homeprod

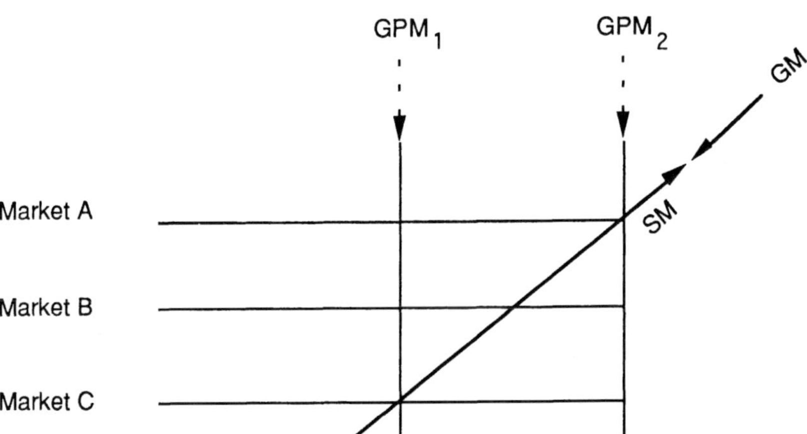

level. For example, a more long-term orientation requires heavy and long-term investments in market positions, something not easily approved by the group. The business of the *Homeprod* subsidiary that was studied has only started to adapt to local conditions. Thus far, the company seems to have been operating in accordance with general group standards similar to those of any other subsidiary within the group. As a result, it has lost both money and a considerable degree of potential expansion during the 1980s. In contrast, another one of the Asian subsidiaries, which has built up its business in a manner adapted to the local conditions just referred to, has been highly successful, a position it has achieved despite strong resistance from the group.

With the group's very large product range, its multi-product line companies tend to develop into mini groups. The local company considered here, for example, consists of nine separate sales units located in three different countries. How such a local group is incorporated locally and what possibilities there are for ownership control and market control of the units depends very much upon the factors of government regulations, the level of corporate citizenship aimed at, and the existence of local partners. The fact that there are three countries involved does not imply this to be a regional company. Quite to the contrary, so as to keep the structure of the group organization flat, the group does not permit there to be organizations having a status between that at the local and at the global level. As a consequence, the group management takes a cautious stance on allowing lateral contacts to take place between sales subsidiaries, particularly if there are such formal arrangements as interlocking directorates. There is thus strong fear of local empires or 'fighting fiefships' developing within the group, something which would make control very difficult in this highly decentralized and geographically dispersed organization with its many different products and companies.

Limited monitoring capacity of the group management

The 'control span' of any given executive in the group seems to be very large. This is a matter which appears in a nutshell to represent the major problem of control for the group. The impression gained from the study is that the group has grown to such a state, mainly through the possibly excessive acquisition of other companies, that the monitoring capacity of the central management of the group is inadequate. This problem is seen especially clearly in the control of subsidiaries in far-off countries differing markedly from the home country, the Asian multi-product line company studied here being an illustrative example. Such companies are directly controlled by group management, at the same time as each subsidiary is small and of marginal importance to the group. In a group organization of this sort there is a preponderance of formal output controls, something which easily becomes too general in a strongly decentralized organization. The risk for 'window-dressing' is great, especially if knowledge regarding the market companies is only superficial at the group level. Such seems to be the case in this group with its many product lines and highly diverse operating companies dispersed throughout the globe. The risk is especially great of group management losing control of its small and remote subsidiaries. Such a flat organizational structure becomes too thin at the periphery, where the kind of informal control and leadership style practised with larger and less remote subsidiaries is not possible. There is a 'black-box syndrome', in which the executive management has too little knowledge regarding the operations of individual companies to be able to control them efficiently. The other side of the matter is that group management easily becomes overloaded with problems. As one of the managing directors who was interviewed remarked: 'a flat organization is always on fire'. The management capacity available may not be sufficient to create common platforms for the organization on the basis of strategic planning. Decisions that are bad from a local subsidiary's standpoint may also be made as was illustrated at the beginning of the book with the case of top management's selling out one product-line company without consulting its multi-divisional subsidiaries in the Far East. Such a control problem seems to be aggravated too by there being a conflict within the organization between a sales culture and a management culture.

Control within the group is thus too homogeneous and differentiated too little in terms of subsidiary type, a matter particularly evident in connection with the group's market subsidiaries here, operating as they are in countries far from group headquarters, countries with market environments and company cultures differing greatly from those in Europe. Flexibility in marketing is important in the region, something which is difficult to achieve in a group such as this, which is still largely production and sales oriented. A better name for the group's product-line companies is perhaps that of 'pipeline companies', since the core of the group's competitive advantage is an efficient combination of production and sales. Large-scale production units supply standard products to a very effective sales force. There now seems to be a change underway, one which will lead to greater flexibility and can be expected to improve the situation for the very specific Asian markets.

A radical solution to the control problems of the group would be to create a regional organization, through moving the executive vice president there to the region, for example. This would increase the direct monitoring of the local companies considerably, but would also tend to reduce the influence which that part of group management still had in Europe, which could have negative effects for the local companies. A critical control issue is thus how the best trade-off of these various aspects can be achieved. There seems to be a slow and gradual change underway here. The present negative economic situation with which the group is faced makes group management particularly receptive to local views. Certain regional functions are also emerging among many of the Eastern Asian subsidiaries. Most of the local subsidiary managers know each other well, since they have been in Asia for a long time and belong to an original group of persons sent there to establish local business. They meet regularly (usually once a year) to discuss common problems. The most important regional function thus established so far is a management training programme.

The chairman of the board of the local subsidiary of prime concern here is an executive vice president from group management. Other members of the board represent the product line companies that have interests connected with the local markets.

The situation for *Homeprod*'s subsidiary in SEA is reminiscent of that with which *Conmine* was confronted earlier before control by the group was improved through increasing the control the product division management could exert. Group control of the *Homeprod* subsidiary in SEA is inefficient, since it is not very responsive to such aspects of the local needs as the specific market situation and business culture. In addition, the monitoring capacity of group management is low. The practice of concentrating on output control is too inefficient and should be combined with better input control and behavioural control so as to reduce transaction costs and improve the group's profitability.

Global Product Organization Separated from a Geographic Organization

Tooltec has two main types of local organization. On the main markets of Europe and the USA the group structure of six product companies (divisions) or business areas is reproduced all the way down to the level of the customer. Each product company is represented by its own sales subsidiary. However, the different subsidiaries operating parallel to one another within the same basic market are owned by a holding company, established within the country in question and owned in turn by the parent company. Hence, there is a clear separation of hierarchical control, on the one hand, and ownership control, on the other. There are two main consolidation and reporting systems, one for each type of fundamental control. Officially, the group is consolidated externally through the holding companies and internally through the product organization.

The other type of local organization is found within the markets such as those in SEA in which the sales of a given division are too small to justify a sales company. Here a local market company represents several divisions and is therefore called a 'multidivisional subsidiary'. Each division active on the market has a 'speaking partner' in the subsidiary, usually a sales manager. Because of the complexity and diversity of the products to be organized within a given division, a single local sales manager is only allowed to handle a maximum of two divisions. However, the local subsidiary manager is responsible for the results there in their entirety. The basic principle behind this local organization of multidivisional subsidiaries is operate in local markets and develop business there by sharing and combining resources, saving overhead costs in this way. For part of the global organization this same principle is also applied on a regional basis. The companies of the different countries within a region share resources with each other through their belonging to a regional company, thus representing a kind of regional minigroup, the region being seen as constituting one single 'company'. The sales of a given division within the whole of the Southeast Asian regional market are often of about the same magnitude as within the market of one of the European countries. The multidivisional subsidiaries are controlled groupwise by a regional company, since they are too small and too numerous to be controlled directly by the product divisions, that instead concentrate on the main markets of real importance. The exerting of lesser control over the regional markets is motivated by their relatively minor sales volume, their lesser degree of development and their very particular character.

Controls

One consequence of this variation in degree of control is that managers from the main product divisions that are active in the region do no more regionally than sit on the regional company board. One major and one minor board meeting takes place each year. The major one, in which the chief executive officer and the group controller also participate, a meeting held somewhere within the region, is more than a board meeting alone. Information on many topics is disseminated, thorough discussions of various problems take place, visits to major customers are made, etc. The regional manager is the representative for the group on the board of the local market companies. In addition, he travels within the region a great deal, something which the regional finance manager and the regional product managers do as well.

Another consequence of this differentiation of control is that the reporting requirements placed on such multidivisional subsidiaries are very much less than it would be for the unidivisional subsidiaries. The main quarterly reporting that is required is much less detailed than it would need to be otherwise. In addition, such subsidiaries need not be linked with the group by means of computers. Largely, there are simply brief official and internal reports. For a regional company such as the one in SEA, the requirements are even less. For instance, sales and financial data are reported for the regional company as a whole, not broken down into those of either the product or the national companies. In one case, this has reduced the requirements on local subsidiary management from their submitting, say, a 27-page report, as a basic market subsidiary in Europe does, to instead submitting 20 lines on a single page in a report on the regional company. The budget is also regional rather than local. A regionally computerized and rather extensive budget and reporting system has been developed to improve regional control. This is a very important control instrument that provides a minimum of constraint and serves as only a basic guideline, the work process itself being more important than the momentary end result.

Strong regional product managers

The regional centre controls a regional warehouse in Singapore and coordinates the support the product divisions provide to individual local subsidiaries. In this way, the direct contacts between Europe and SEA are reduced considerably. Support is handled by regional product managers, sent out by and paid for by the divisions. They are normally based at the centre in Singapore, but may also be placed within the local market company, where such a responsibility may also be combined with that of being the manager for the local subsidiary as a whole. Such a regional product manager provides technical support to the local sales companies, which is vital in selling technically advanced products, support which the individual sales companies normally cannot afford. These experts are not part of the formal hierarchical control system, since they have only supportive and consultative roles, their dealing with such problems, for example, as transfer pricing and the coordination of supplies. They have influence but no formal control authority. The local subsidiary manager, who is responsible for local sales, reports to the regional manager. Thus, 'local subsidiary managers cannot be pushed around by the regional product managers', at least not according to the formal structure of authority. Control also takes place through informal communication and cross-departmental relations. The line of demarcation between this kind of control and control by formal authority is a fluid one. A strong and well-established local subsidiary manager 'who knows everyone in the group' may attempt to take advantage of this situation by bypassing the regional product manager and dealing directly with the product division in Europe, for example in trying to negotiate a better transfer price. This is normally not formally allowed by company rules, the minimum requirement under such conditions being that the regional product manager be notified. To avoid situations of this sort, the regional product managers have been given a more active role, especially in the regional budgeting process, in which they are to decide on future programmes of action together with the local product managers.

Constructive dissent of this sort is viewed as dealing in a constructive way with conflict between global product interests and local market interests. Information for final decisions regarding the budget is obtained from two sources: the local subsidiary managers and the regional manager. This arrangement also reduces the traditionally strong position which local subsidiary managers have, its rather being the regional product manager who is given the key role in bridging the gap between local market interests and global product interests. This is of particular importance in a situation of increasing competition such as existed in SEA at the end of the 1980s, when it was important to increase control of local business due to products being so difficult to sell. Under more normal conditions too, however, managers within the local subsidiaries need to be influenced from outside to change their locally-oriented thinking of readily referring to the domestic culture as an excuse for not following group strategies. At the same time, regional product managers fresh on the job often have too little understanding of the local situation. Attitudes such as this are common: 'This product has successfully been sold in this way everywhere in the world, so why not in Southeast Asia?' The important process here of accommodating two disparate perspectives is gradual and slow.

The division of sales work between local sales branches, sales subsidiaries and the regional level of the organization varies a great deal but also has important commonalities, for example being strongly influenced by the local dimension and often hard to comprehend at the divisional headquarters in Europe. In some countries there is a combination of multi-salesmen who mainly handle customer contacts, of product specialists at sales subsidiaries, and of technical experts at the regional office. The general principle within the group of having product-specialized salesmen does not always work.

An important conclusion to be drawn is that a regional company can improve control of local business considerably (see Figure 5.5).The vertical linkage problem can be solved in a more efficient way through the intermediary role of the regional product manager, at the same time as horizontal coordination is furthered, for example by means of the regional manager or the regional budget system. The *Tooltec* case illustrates the fact that within the transnational M-form a regional organization can provide a highly efficient means of improving control. Control in the *Tooltec* case by group management located

Figure 5.5 Main conflicts of interest at Tooltec

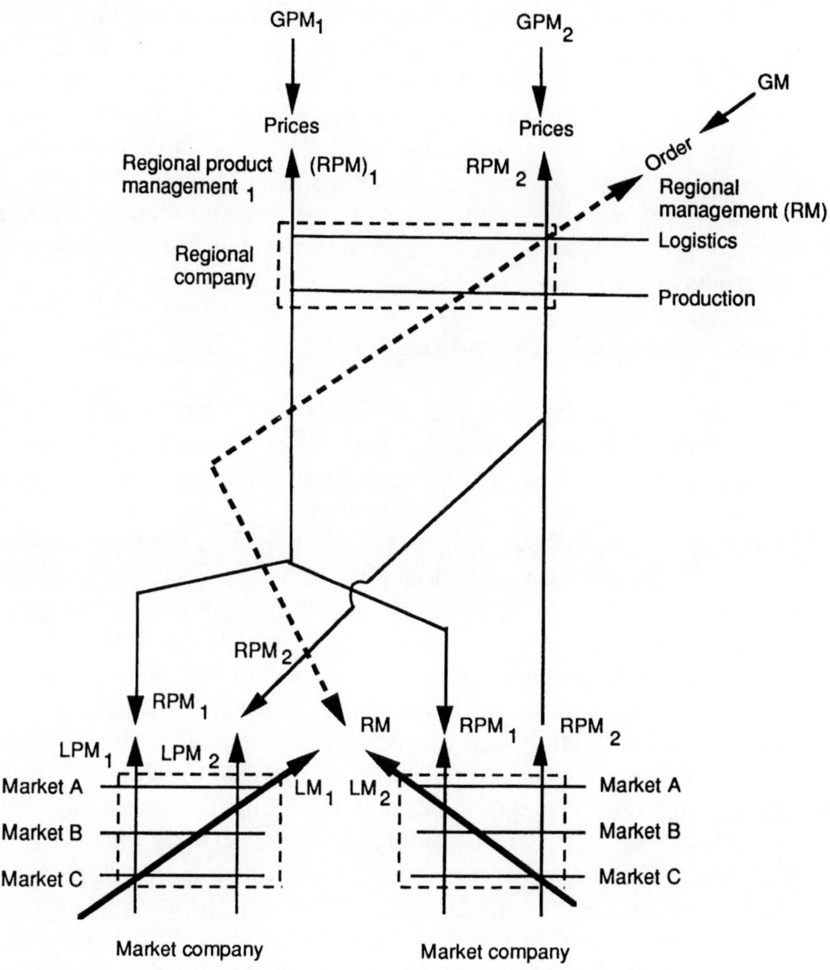

centrally has been reduced, at the same time as a form of groupwise regional control of subsidiaries in SEA has been established. To this end, certain members of group management from Europe have been assigned to the region. The advantages of this in terms of information costs can be clearly seen, there being a trade-off between reduction in requirements regarding the submission of reports to the group and an increase in requirements regarding submission of reports to the regional office, something which has been done for the product divisions as well. Vertical control has been transferred to the region through giving product experts authority by allowing them a leading role in a major form of output control – the budgeting process. The local product interests found at the subsidiaries are best controlled by the regional representative of global product interests, something which also reduces enforcement costs. In addition, control of the local interests which the local subsidiary manager represents is enhanced by the presence of a regional product manager, bargaining costs being reduced, for example, through it being more difficult for the local subsidiary manager to act in an opportunistic way by circumventing the regional company so as to negotiate transfer prices directly with the product divisions.

Pure Global Product Organization

Particularly, conditions that prevailed in Asian markets called attention for the first time to certain weaknesses in *Trans*' worldwide organization. After a number of years, it was realized that the degree of responsibility assigned to the group's regional company in Singapore for sales of the group's major products in Eastern Asia was more than that company could handle, since the company's limited management resources were spread too thinly, involving too many products. There was too little concentration on the major business in the area, something true also of the distributors, who were given too little support and were too independent. There was insufficient coordination of marketing as it related to customers, the market organization not being focused on the customer sufficiently. There were no 'straight pipelines' through the organization directly into the market. Poor coordination between production and marketing was another weakness. The manufacturing units established in the area were located in a parallel organization that was controlled too much by the main factory located in Europe, therefore being very little involved in marketing and distribution. The products assembled locally were delivered to the distributors directly. In addition, a strong and resistant tradition of production thinking was found within the group, something which was hard to change to a more definite market orientation within the organization. This largely functional and horizontal organization, in which the different parts of the value chain were separated from each other, was too much a copy of the organization found in the group (see Figure 5.6).

Figure 5.6 Main conflicts of interest at Trans

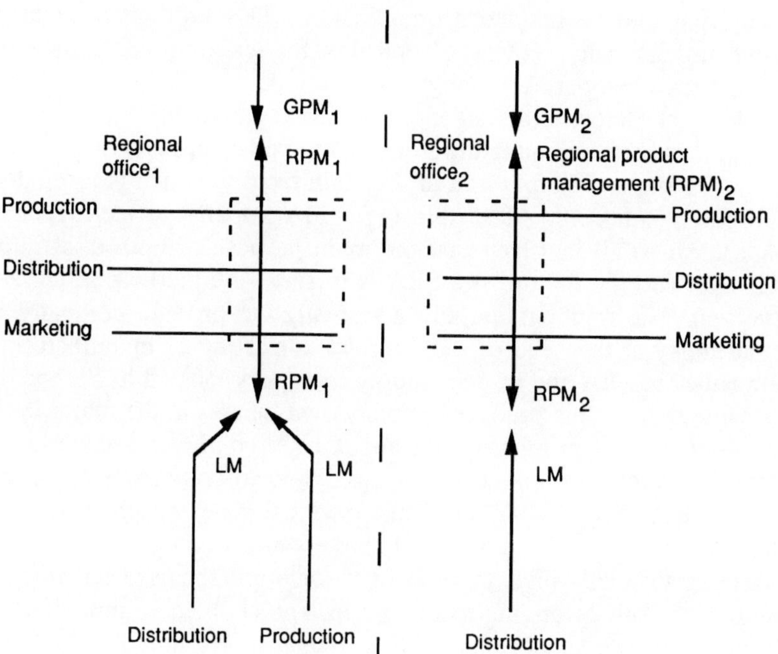

Improved vertical integration

To increase vertical coordination along the value chain, the regional organization was segmented in accordance with the product type into two regional companies: one having total responsibility for the main product and the other having responsibility for two products sold in the area. This has increased the market orientation in the whole organization considerably through making customers the starting point within the vertical product segments. To achieve this, distributors in the various SEA countries were divided up among the two regional product companies. This has made it easier to integrate them into the group's logistic system, which is a critical factor in this type of industry. It is also important for another reason, namely that some dealers also represent competing products, often Japanese competitors which are very strong in the area. In addition, the dealers often belong to large business groups. The contacts of each of the regional companies with the distributors are organized functionally throughout the region, the after-sales people of a regional company dealing with after-sales people of the distributors, and so forth. This means that a given *Trans* unit and a given distributor with which it deals have counterparts in each other's organization. This facilitates contacts between them. Such improved control of the distributors has increased the firm's competitive strength.

The local factories in Asia are assigned to the main regional company, all of them manufacturing the same type of product. Moreover, the packaging and supply unit of the main factory, which is located in Europe, is subordinated to this regional company, it having been made clear to all involved that the main purpose of both this European unit and the factories in SEA is to serve the markets which are involved. The regional, largely administrative product company is found today at the head of a minigroup consisting of manufacturing companies in SEA and of one 'supply' company located in Europe, at the same time as this product company owns shares in the major local distributors. This minigroup has about 1000 employees. In order to minimize administrative costs, the two regional companies share the same office, which can also be used by other product groups interested in investigating regional markets or investing there. In such a case as this, in which there are two or more separate but related companies both belonging to the group, one of them is appointed to be the 'corporate spokesman'. This makes it responsible for the horizontal coordination of the two regional companies and for representing the group as a whole, for instance in dealings with local governments. This assignment is usually given to the largest regional company, but may also be given to the company with the managing director of highest seniority.

A few years after, a global product organization of this type, which was tried out initially in Eastern Asia, was completely implemented in the group as a whole. Such a transition was expedited by a close cooperation with another large European TNC within the same industry. Each product company of the group is now geographically organized in a way modelled after the experience gained in Asia. The regional company primarily considered in this study now belongs to a larger region basically comprising those parts of the world other than two major European regions and the USA.

Controls

Representation on the board of the regional company is the most important form of ownership control within the group. Places on the board are therefore occupied by different representatives of the product company. These include one vice president from the executive management group in Europe, the regional director who is based in Europe, and one person from the main European factory, along with the managing director of the supply company in Europe, the managing director of a group company in another part of Asia, the managing director of one regional company, and the managing director of the other regional company in the area. Since the last position named is held by a local, the government rule of having one local representative on the board is fulfilled. Ownership control in the region is also maintained, the managing director of the regional company being the chairman of the board of the manufacturing companies in the region at the same time as he is also a member of the boards of the major distributors.

This new product organization has improved the control of the regional units. Clear and unambiguous objectives, easy to measure and communicate have now been expressed. Employees throughout the organization are more motivated, since they can better see the link between effort and sales performance. A budget system and an information and reporting system which were already good have been improved through data communication, permanent telephone lines and a memo system. Good communications are vital because of the large distances within the region and between there and Europe. Even if a need might be felt for more than four board meetings a year, this can scarcely be achieved due to the large distances involved. The same goes for the regional company's executive management group, which comprises persons from different parts of the region as well as one person who is based in Europe, who likewise cannot meet in person as often as might be desirable.

Whereas the *Tooltec* case illustrates how in a vertically segmented organization the regional organization can improve the horizontal coordination found at a local level, the *Trans* case demonstrates the opposite, namely how the inefficiency of a horizontally segmented organization can be improved by vertical segmentation and coordination of the organization, including its regional functions. Inefficiencies in decision making (high information costs), in the implementation of decisions for markets and distributors (enforcement costs), and those due to conflicts between units within the region and outside (bargaining costs) are reduced by rearranging major controls from horizontal to vertical control of the organization.

Adding a new product division

Indcomp's regional organization in SEA has been completely reorganized recently and has been divisionalized in accordance with the group organization. First, those business units belonging to the major after market (AM) division were separated from those belonging to one of the minor divisions. At the same time, each of the main operations was specialized and was organized in a separate company. The AM division within SEA now consists of sales companies in various of the countries, a 'supply' company centred in Singapore and responsible for logistics and for the central warehouse, and a 'distributor' company also located in Singapore and responsible for establishing and managing new and small distributors. The larger and more mature distributors are managed directly by the local sales companies. These local companies within the AM-division are assigned to the regional office, which represents group management within the region, and also has major support and staff functions. The regional office can likewise be used by new business areas during their period of becoming established, a matter described in some detail below for the case of the original equipment market (OEM) division. This case in question also demonstrates the fact that it is comparatively easy to add new product divisions to a divisionalized organization, particularly if the overall product division is large and plays a central role within the group. The problems illustrated above in the cases of *Conmine* and of *Match* are less here since a division with ample resources can establish an organization of its own.

Indcomp is the market leader in its field of business with Western Europe and North America. However, it is far from being in such a position in Eastern Asia, since this is the 'hemisphere' in which Japanese companies are dominant. Competition has made it particularly costly to seize the high volumes inherent in selling directly to equipment manufacturers. It is very hard to 'break into' relationships which have been built up between Japanese manufacturers and suppliers from both Japan and SEA. This TNC's initial strategy, therefore, was to concentrate on the low-volume industrial AM, in which several thousand product varieties are sold mostly through external parties or distributors. Marketing to the AM is carried out by one of the five separate business areas or divisions within the group. This division is called here the AM division, a term already referred to above. The marketing, production and distribution of components to the original equipment market is by far the largest business area of the group, called here the OEM division. In recent years *Indcomp* has also taken up this main area of business regionally within SEA, a separate sales organization and a large factory have been established there. Whereas the product managers of that sales organization are located at the regional area office in Singapore, the regional factory is located in a neighbouring country.

There are marked differences between these two divisions which now operate within the region. The AM division sells a wide variety of different small-volume components indirectly to a large number of industries and other customers, whereas the OEM division sells and manufactures a few large-volume components directly to a limited number of large customers in a few industries. Economies of scale are of paramount importance for the latter division but are not to the same extent for the former, which is sales and distribution-oriented. The OEM division is production-oriented, a major marketing task being to link two production systems with each other, one at the supplier end and one at the customer end. Sales activity as such is not that important, and is more a question of having a long-term competitive price, of adhering to the delivery dates, and of maintaining high and consistent quality. These advantages are created for the most part by efficient production, whereas efficient distribution and good customer relationships are the basis of the competitive strength of the AM division. The production-orientation of the dominant OEM division also tends to spill over to other divisions. This main difference manifests itself in many ways. When OEM built up its sales organization in SEA most of the market information available within the more regionally experienced AM division could not be used, since it was organized in terms of customers and not of products.

The AM division

The local market activities of the distributors within the AM are controlled in two ways. The major objective is to control the distributors directly and on the spot through the establishment of own sales subsidiaries. This provides a better knowledge of the local market, improved possibilities for the firm's implementing its own policies towards the distributors, and makes it easier to support the latter, and to obtain direct contact with the final customers. The local presence of sales people, of stock and of administration is seen as vital. This has been achieved within the larger markets, whereas distributors within the smaller markets are controlled from a separate 'distributor' company located in Singapore. When a market has been built up sufficiently to allow for it, a sales subsidiary is established and distributors are transferred as well. The new subsidiary is subordinated to the regional headquarters instead of to the regional distributor company. Partnerships with distributors are formalized in contracts, the degree of exclusiveness of distributorship varying and determining the degree of control. The basic principle, however, is that the products which *Indcomp* offers are to be the most competitive and therefore the most attractive available to distributors. The more attractive products are, the greater the extent to which hierarchical types of control can be replaced by market control. Positive controls such as incentives are thus more important than negative controls.

Locating business activities close to customers is vital, since *Indcomp* stresses high quality as its main competitive tool, and as the justification for its higher and less competitive prices. This is made possible through a strong local presence and a superior distribution network. Close proximity is necessary in order to implement a marketing strategy based on technical discussions and the training of distributors and customers. Making products available in the region through the presence of a broad distribution network is more important in SEA than in Europe in order that the times of delivery promised can be kept. The central warehouse in Singapore is thus mandatory for a regional logistics system to function efficiently, the importance of such operations being manifested by the fact that the logistics of the firm are organized as a separate company.

Pricing is also considerably more sophisticated in the AM than in the original equipment market, since the types of products, customers, and industries are much greater in number. A major aim of the marketing policy is to come closer to the final customers in order to provide solutions to their needs. This has become more and more important with the extension of the AM division's marketing concept. Earlier, the company focused on limited customer needs related to selling and servicing certain high-quality components. Now, the focus is on solving the customers' logistical problems involving transportation, storage, and the end-user's production and process results. The company is abandoning its basic strategy of being a product specialist so as to become more of a customer specialist. To accomplish this, *Indcomp* needs to extend its product range even more and concentrate much more on maintenance provided as a service. Close cooperation with final customers also requires closer cooperation with distributors, the company and its distributors operating as a team in their contacts with the end-users. *Indcomp* is thus increasing its investments in the distribution network.

Controls

Indcomp's group organization is decentralized, the staff at group headquarters, for example, having been slimmed down considerably. Output control, chiefly by means of the budget system, is the most important control strategy for all divisions within the group. The basis of this control is a computerized and highly advanced budget and reporting system which makes it possible to consolidate the group every month, there being one reporting system for internal and one for external purposes. This emphasis on output control is an expression of a policy of measuring organizational behaviour as much as possible. However, there seems to be a bias towards internal measures rather than maintaining close control of competitors. An important basis for this system and for other activities, such as marketing, for example, is a very advanced internal transfer price system. It is a critical element, since it connects all the units and vital functions of the group such as production, distribution, marketing and finance. Such a system is particularly important in a mature industry of global character, which *Indcomp* indeed represents. Internal prices are fixed for one year at a time and are based on annual negotiations between group units. Such factors as market demand, production volumes in the factories producing the various types of components, and exchange rate developments are considered here.

This budget and reporting system also works as an 'intricate' rule-oriented process control mechanism. Rules, as embodied in sales manuals, programmes or manuals for distributors, represent an important form of information control. Lateral relations achieved through temporary or permanent teams, task forces, committees, integrators, or integrative departments are not particularly important in a vertical and heavily formal organization such as *Indcomp*'s, but there is a need for a different type of lateral organization, that of informal communication which serves as an information control, especially through hastening decisions and the implementation of them. This does not mean that such formal controls as output control or information control through rules can be evaded, but only that they allow a flexibility that can be taken advantage of through a communication network of this sort, one for which there is a need even within an organization of this type with its heavy formal controls.

'Management by travelling around' is an important form of information control through the building and maintaining of an informal communication network, as well as of direct behaviour control and of input control through the process of socialization in which regional management becomes acquainted with global management's way of thinking. The chief executive of the AM division, for instance, travels during two-thirds of his working days each year. Such behaviour serves as a 'role model' for other executives and readily leads to an increase in their travel time. The advice they provide and the dialogue in which they are engaged during their travels represent important aspects of information control.

Input control is a highly important form of control at many levels of *Indcomp*'s group organization. Socialization and the building of a corporate culture is mainly carried out informally, as exemplified above, and also by such means as the arranging of trips to specific places for groups of employees from a unit. Top management in certain divisions has begun recently to pay more attention to company culture. Attempts have also been made to capture specific as well as more implicit aspects of the company culture that has evolved over the years. There are large differences in company culture between the two main business areas. Formulating missions and focusing on common values constitute attempts at input control. However, such efforts do not seem as yet to have penetrated the organization very deeply. Until quite recently there were few management training programmes carried out within the group, human resource management being largely centralized in group headquarters in Europe, where matters concerning the expatriates within the group are dealt with.

One main conclusion to be drawn from the *Indcomp* case is that, when two dissimilar product divisions are involved, it can be quite effective to differentiate controls vertically and to control activities throughout the entire vertical value chain, all the way to the customer. However, the case also illustrates the fact that certain controls, for example rules and output control, can achieve a high degree of standardization, and that it may be sensible to extend the organization of the product division to the regional and local levels if the need for this is sufficient.

MULTIDIMENSIONAL ORGANIZATION

Telecom was indicated in Chapter 3 to be the only example here of a multidimensional organization. How this organization came about as a consequence of problems experienced within the global product organization was described. The need for an organization of this type in such remote markets as Australia and SEA emerged early. A regional organization was seen as being an important concept within a multidimensional organization as a means of attaining a kind of critical mass in terms of the size of operations and for improving horizontal communication between the various local companies. The group has now gained considerable experience with the regional organization form in SEA which has been useful for the group as a whole. As will be discussed in Chapter 6, *Telecom* had a regional office first in Bangkok and then in Singapore for several years. The basic reason for the move to Singapore was to be able to use the latter office for the company as a whole. However, as will be discussed in that chapter, the regional concept has mainly been applied to a given business area, within which a high regional coordination has been aimed at. With such a regional organization, which allocates resources, local strategic capabilities can be improved, at the same time as the local organization increases its strength, both on the local market and within the group. In this way, a regional organization can be a forerunner for the new multidimensional group organization that is based on achieving a balance between corporate, product divisional and local levels and on an increase in horizontal coordination. Since a regional office's main function is to coordinate, it can easily extend this task to other product divisions. This is also something which is starting to happen in SEA.

In a multidimensional organization it could be more efficient to locate regional functions in local subsidiaries than in a regional administrative centre, concerning for example the technical capacity there to develop bids for small and medium-sized projects. On the whole, there seems to be a tendency within *Telecom* to locate regional facilities in individual local subsidiaries rather than collecting facilities at a regional office.

A multidimensional organization tends to be suitable for selling and managing large projects which require a high degree of flexibility and a large informal network organization. However, the economy of local subsidiaries cannot be built on the basis of project business alone, such business serving more as a complement to basic bread and butter sales. An informal network-type organization is important for a multidimensional organization to have, but it must be anchored within the formal organization in order to create the proper framework for the informal organization and its control to function.

One reason for *Telecom*'s having the high degree of differentiation and the flexibility locally which it possesses is the presence of its many agents in SEA, these agents being managed by the local subsidiaries, often very informally, most of them not having any formal linkages to the product divisions or to group management.

CONCLUSIONS

Transactions carried on in distant Southeast Asian countries were incorporated into five of the six main types of transnational group structure presented in Chapter 3. These patterns for global organization differ in their responsiveness to local conditions, in their facility for integrating transactions worldwide, and their ability to balance local and global interests. This partly reflects their differing in the limits they set through the use of controls. The decentralized spatial M-form, the control of which is based on socialization and on performance control, the control here relying both on high powered incentives and on administrative processes, possesses a high degree of efficiency. This form of organization can be seen as an intermediary that combines the best of two different systems: the traditional hierarchy and the market.

In a fully-fledged global product organization, each market company tends to be assigned to a specific product company, resulting in several different market companies at the group located in any given country, each representing a different product company. In small markets, however, such an organization is inefficient, due to the establishment costs of the specialist structures involved. In addition, for local customers it is a disadvantage to have to meet with several different representatives of a given group rather than simply with one. Therefore, a group is usually represented by market companies, the mixture of product companies involved varying with different market companies. Market companies are connected to a group in different ways. In one form of organization, they are 'sliced' up among the various product companies, whereas in another they are assigned to the largest product company present at the local level. In still another, such market companies are separated from the rest of the organization and are subordinated to the general management. In the last form, a mother-daughter type structure can be said to exist within the transnational organization. This easily leads to decisions being inferior from a global standpoint because of the low degree of control by group management. The low degree of control results in transaction costs being higher and accordingly in considerable risk for suboptimization and a lowering of profits.

Although the freedom of action of the market companies in the region varies, it is still comparatively large, the need for responsiveness to local conditions usually being higher in these distant markets with their highly specific characteristics. Controls developed for business activities in Western Europe, for example, might well be unfit in SEA or have to be executed differently. This appeared to be the case for many of the TNCs that were studied. The fast growth of East Asian markets has created a mismatch between the global and local levels. The mixed subsidiaries, in particular, could be better integrated into the group if there were a more open attitude in Europe towards these very special markets and a greater appreciation of their special needs and requirements. The specific circumstances under which these subsidiaries exist need to be considered to a greater extent so as to make it possible for group management and/or product group management to control them better and thereby increase profits for the group as a whole. These subsidiaries constitute the final test of the transnational orientation of a TNC. They pose the question of how best to differentiate control so as to take adequate account both of these minor but fast-growing markets and the major but stagnating mature markets in Europe, and bridge the large institutional gap between organizations in Europe and in Asia.

The local competitive situation of the TNCs that were studied is one highly specific to Eastern Asia. It involves a dominance of the own sales companies of a group rather than of external parties, as well as a high degree of internal organization locally as compared with many of their transnational competitors. This is a consequence of the high-technological profile of these TNCs, which manifested itself in a global product interest being dominant. The competitive strength of these firms is based on high product quality, training and service. The strategy of maintaining this in an environment characterized by stiff price competition, low technical levels and a lack of long-term investment thinking demands an extensive transfer of technology and the presence of technical expertise which is organized internally.

Another reason for the internalization of operations in SEA is the need for a high degree of responsiveness to the local environment, something which has been shown throughout the book. This involves links to many different parties in the local market through investments. At the same time, the need for high adaptability to the circumstances of these very specific markets involves a strong conflict between global product interests and local interests. In the one-dimensional global product organization, this conflict tends to be solved at the expense of the local interests. A more efficient control of such conflict can be achieved in a multi-dimensional organization, one in which geographic dimension is not treated as basically less important than the global product dimension. A formal matrix organization, on the other hand, does not seem to be a realistic option. Some of the TNCs had had bad experience with an organization of this sort earlier, and others were aware of its bad reputation, for example its excessive conflicts and unclear lines of command. Thus, even if conflict between local and global perspectives cannot be avoided, it can scarcely be considered a good idea to formalize it in a matrix organization. What seems to be necessary for achieving a transnational solution is to give the two major organizational dimensions of a TNC just referred to an equal standing, at the same time as the emphasis in more traditional organizational forms is in a sense reversed by taking the local markets as the point of departure, such as was done in the *Telecom* case. In the multidimensional organization the trade-off between these two principles is a highly differentiated one, the controls varying considerably from one type of activity to another. An increased emphasis on the geographic dimension in general would most certainly raise bargaining costs, but this could be more than compensated for by a reduction in the information and enforcement costs through the more differentiated controls.

To the TNCs referred to in the cases discussed above, such markets as those in SEA are still of marginal importance to the group as a whole, the impact of these markets on the organizational structure of the groups in question often not being particularly great. Possible inefficiencies reflected in large transaction costs, through creating slack, may nevertheless prevail. The world organization of such a firm is still indeed primarily based on the firm's business in the industrialized countries of Western Europe and North America, in other markets that are more remote being less integrated into the overall framework. In such cases it may be seen as non-economical to try to reduce very much the inefficiency which is found. This makes it impossible for a complete fit between a market company and group structure to be achieved for a subsidiary in an industrially developing country. Certain of the reasons for this are as follows:

1. A small market volume can be seen as constituting too limited a foundation for decomposing an organization into separate product companies or separate distribution and production units.
2. Specific circumstances such as legislation, cultural matters, or type of marketing and production may make a market company unfit for group structure. The interest a group has in a market

company situated in a country in which majority ownership may even be disallowed and other such problems may exist, is likely to be less than its interest in countries to which it feels more akin. If a market company is considered more as an affiliated company than as a subsidiary, it may be more efficient to externalize transactions.

3. Group structure may be unfit for the structure of a particular market company. For example, the international organization of the concern may be too constrained, and too much determined by the home market.

The study suggests that when business in markets such as those in SEA becomes more essential to a group, interest in these markets will increase, facilitating the integration of those markets, particularly the product companies into the group. Subsidiaries in such areas will then be taken more seriously. This will reflect partly the rapid increase in their importance and partly the fact of the group in question gradually coming to terms with the problems found there, thus being able to integrate these subsidiaries more and more into their future world business. For *Trans, Indpow, Telecom*, and *Pills*, business in Asia is already of considerable importance to the group and the subsidiaries in the area are well integrated into the group organization. The local organization in SEA of two of these groups has also had a vital impact on the global organization of the group.

NOTES

1. See Hedlund and Åhman (1984).
2. See Hedlund (1984, p. 119).

6. Local Organization

This chapter considers global structures in which the geographical dimension dominates, but in which the product dimension also plays an important role. The local organization of TNCs that have a global organization involving various regional structures is analysed first. In such TNCs, the 'divisionalization' of group structure into regions tends to be found throughout the organization, from the centre out to the level of the local markets. Two cases are presented to illustrate this type of TNC.

Another type with a strong geographic basis is of the mother-daughter variety. This type of organization is represented, among the organizations examined in the present book, by various of the smaller TNCs, as well as by certain of the larger TNCs with very limited operations in SEA. Matrix organization is uncommon among such TNCs and is only found in one of them.

Local organization involves matters of regional organization as well, various forms of which were analysed in Chapter 5. In this chapter, the matter of regional organization of TNCs as it relates to local organization in SEA is analysed in greater detail, along with the question of how an ordinary sales organization is combined with a project organization at the local level.

An additional matter taken up in the chapter is that of the organization of transfer pricing, something which has a marked impact on the independence of subsidiaries located in SEA. It is a key to the maintenance of control by the European TNC as was seen in Chapter 2. An important finding reported earlier (Jansson, 1993) was that, irrespective of group organization, market companies in SEA have a greater freedom of action in deciding about customer prices than they do about transfer prices. The main reason for this seems to be the relatively small size of these market companies compared with the size of their groups. A further observation that can be made, one that will be discussed below, is that by being organized in their approach to pricing through a regional company, the SEA subsidiaries of a TNC can increase their chances of influencing transfer prices, although the cost accounting system of the group may considerably limit the effects of such efforts.

REGIONAL STRUCTURES

Pills' group organization is organized functionally, the marketing organization being further sub-divided along geographical lines. The Americas represent one region, whereas in Europe there are four regions, and in the Asian-Pacific area there are three. Regional structures are not uncommon for the pharmaceutical industry (Robock and Simmonds, 1989, p. 264). The Asian region studied here is the second largest in economic terms in the Asian-Pacific area after Japan. The regional division of the organization is a reflection of a major strategic change toward the end of the 1970s, when it was decided to concentrate on the core business, which meant focusing on certain segments of the industry and certain geographical areas. Thus, the group divested itself of its activities in certain product segments and geographical areas, largely pulling out of South America through licensing away its products there and replacing its own sales companies with agents.

The regional administrative office for the region of Asia examined here, which comprises most of South and East Asia, is situated in Singapore. It is the headquarters for the sales companies of the group located within the major markets of the region, for its distributors to minor markets and to markets within which TNC subsidiaries are not allowed, as well as for two companies affiliated with the group. Two important markets within which the group has been established for many years fall outside of this organization, namely those of Japan and of one of the other Asian countries. The regional office just referred to is a profits centre and has total responsibility for the group's business in the region. There is also a service and marketing support centre at this office. The R. & D. companies in Europe place persons of their own in positions of being marketing managers for the region, so as to support the sales companies and the distributors there. This creates an important link between marketing in the region and the R. & D. located in Europe. Coordination of activities in the whole region tends to be necessary for a critical mass to be obtained in terms of operations. The regional organization also allows a cross-fertilization between units to be achieved through joint management meetings, marketing activities and training. An essential activity in this particular industry is clinical research. This is managed by a separate medical department at the regional centre. There is also a separate regional financial controller at this office. The regional centre is a catalyst and facilitating means for organizational development, product flow, collaboration and coordination, primarily between and within the local markets but also between them and for Asian companies outside the region.

The regional strategy that *Pills* has adapted to the Asia region can be implemented most efficiently through its own organization. This is partly due to various characteristics of the markets and marketing processes for the products sold in the area. The markets are heterogeneous and fragmented and there are both international and local competitors. There is a very strong focus on marketing to physicians, which is best carried out through an own sales organization. The kind of concentrated marketing required cannot, therefore, be successfully handled by agents. Relationships characterized by trust are essential in dealing with this customer group. These can best be achieved by the own sales force. The types of marketing goals pursued add to this, goals of high volume growth and high relative market shares (penetration), goals vital to an industry dominated by extremely high costs for R. & D. and for product development. If distributors are nevertheless utilized, it is essential that their costs and pricing be controlled through maintaining the company presence and through remaining in close contact with the distributors. Thus, a control of external parties similar to that of the internal sales organization needs to be aimed at. Also, it is essential that clinical research be part of the own organization in order that control of the process of approval of products by the local authorities can be maintained, such research likewise representing an important basis for marketing. In addition, competitive strength in the pharmaceutical industry very much rests on intangible assets which a company possesses, particularly those involving such intellectual property as patents and trade-marks. The protection of these assets varies considerably between the different Asian countries. Copying is a well-known fact of life in the industry, particularly in Asia. Large domestic industries have even been built up in some countries through such means. Combatting such factors requires a strong local presence, one which can only be achieved through an own organization.

The specific competitive situation prevailing in East Asia requires, therefore, an intimate knowledge of customers, competitors and authorities, as well as having the right connections with the system. A true insider position is necessary, something which also places certain demands on the internal organization. For instance, it is extremely important to find able locals to serve as managing directors for the sales companies. There is a clear connection between company performance and the local savvy and acceptability of the person selected for this position. In the broad framework established by the group, this person matters very much, particularly in view of the highly decentralized nature of the sales organization, where it is up to the local company to optimize the product mix and other marketing variables. On the whole, this policy has worked well, among other things due to the entrepreneurial drive and favourable work ethics evident in the region (these can be considered important local factors). Expatriates are less suitable for such a job, since they do not stay in the region long enough and since they are exposed to many of the problems typically encountered by foreigners. All the country managers except one are nationals.

The regional group has been very successful during its first decade of operations. The turnover of goods has increased elevenfold, the contribution to group results 35 times, and the number of employees has quadrupled to a present 300. Growth has been both rapid and steady. This has been achieved with the use of a well-balanced portfolio of products of varied historical age, involving all of the main products of the group, and with excellent sales within all market segments of high priority. In most cases too, a lead position has been achieved in the local market. The local resources built up have been more than adequate and the physical distribution has functioned efficiently, the regional office maintaining full control in all countries of high priority. The region is on a par with any major European company within the group when it comes to registration and launching of *Pills*' priority products, and the product turnover of this regional group is larger for its size than for the TNC's regional groups in the world generally. A ranking of the major corporations within the pharmaceutical industry in the Asian region shows *Pills* to generally be found in the range of ranks 10-20 as compared with a range of 30-40 for the world at large, although the group's regional ranking in Europe is higher yet. Marketing research also shows that *Pills* can now, for its size and for the sector of the overall Asian market it represents, be considered as very well known in Asia. A consistent and long-term marketing strategy for the past ten years is surely one main factor behind this success. Such a strategy is also well-suited to the business culture of the area. However well-established *Pills* is in the region, it has not yet reached the position of being a major contributor to the overall group in terms of sales and earnings. That is a major future objective.

The regional director reports to the head of the Asian region in Europe, who is a member of the executive management group, whereas the other regional directors report directly to the CEO. This reporting is done formally on a monthly basis. The responsibility for the regional budget and for setting local objectives has been decentralized to the region, but decisions there need to be approved by the executive unit in accordance with the group's two-year planning and budget system.

Figure 6.1 Pills' *local organization*

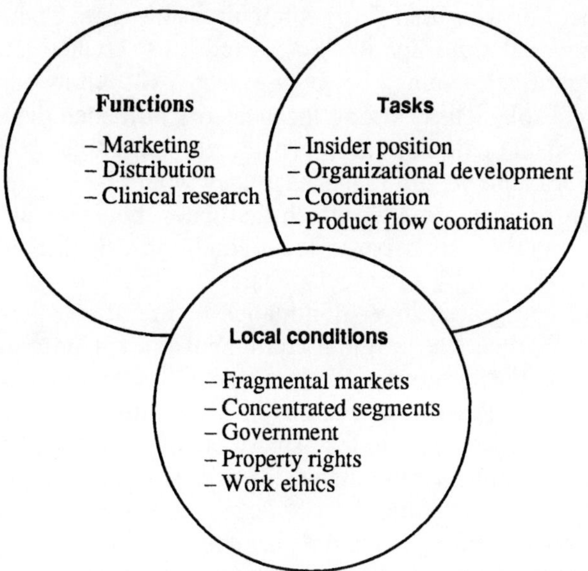

Pills' local organization is summarized schematically in Figure 6.1. The local conditions that are listed in the table readily engender strong local interest in the company and provide reasons for the regional transactions being separated from those of the group's. These local conditions also affect transactions in a specific way, making it efficient to internalize transactions and control them through a suitable mix of ownership, and of market and hierarchical control. It is particularly important to control the implementation of decisions regarding marketing, distribution and clinical research, in view of the weak protection of property rights within the region. An own organization is vital to provide for control of enforcement and information costs, both of which are reduced by having an insider position. Bargaining costs are mainly controlled through the strong decentralization in the organization and through the careful selection process followed in the placing of managing directors in the local companies.

MOTHER-DAUGHTER ORGANIZATION

As was observed in earlier chapters, *Wear and Tear* is represented by one centrally-located subsidiary in East Asia. This company's international organization was also classified earlier as being of the mother-daughter type. For *Wear and Tear,* continuity is the main characteristic of its customer relationships in SEA, where trust created and maintained by repetitive meetings between persons who know each other plays a critical role. These strong local factors influence the regional organization of the company here considerably. Contract periods for expatriates, for example, are longer than they would be for these same individuals in Europe, a matter which facilitates the subsidiary in the region being highly responsive to local conditions. Such responsiveness is also influenced by a particular characteristic of markets in SEA, namely there being a stronger dominance of the after-sales market there than in Europe, the original-equipment market dominating in Europe. The parent company was not conscious of this difference during its first five years of operations in SEA. This led among other things to marked differences in the assessment of the subsidiary's performance in the region. Group management meant that local management tended to simply blame the Chinese business culture there and differences between European and Asian countries for their not being able to implement the parent company's marketing strategies in the region. There was too much central control. This situation has gradually changed and the local marketing strategies adopted have proven to be profitable. The real turnaround came with a change in parent company management. The regional market subsidiary there is much more independent today and has its own sales strategies. The parent company's confidence in local management is also much greater than before.

Local management has also learnt increasingly about how to operate in the area and control business operations. On the whole, this has meant that the company has become more Chinese in its outlook. The principle of Yin and Yang is seen as the major principle for strategy and for the organization of regional business, its being seen as critical that harmony be created in various ways. This principle penetrates the entirety of the organization locally, from the basics of the sales organization to the smallest details, such as the colour of the office curtains and the layout of the office (Feng Shui). Efficient control in terms of the Yin-Yang principle involves achieving the right balance between the external and internal sales organization. It was shown, for example, that the use of agents gave the wrong balance. There was too little control of sales since agents concentrated on those products, either products of the company or products of competitors, that had the best profit potential in the short term. The agent in one of the markets created bad-will for the company, in fact, something it took years to recover from. In addition, the agents provided the customers with no technical support. A better balance and a more long-term orientation was achieved by the company's establishing its own representative offices in the main markets and replacing agents with distributors. The internal organization has thus been extended forwards into the market and the company has come closer to its customers. The main task of the regional subsidiary is now to provide technical support and, together with distributors, to influence customers. This means creating a better balance between two main marketing tasks: those of technical support and of more commercial aspects of sales and distribution. Since customers tend to trust technicians more than salesmen, a better balance has also been achieved in this respect. It has been seen as important to maintain the distinction between these two main types of company representatives and to hinder technicians from interfering with the commercial aspects of business as well as vice versa.

This extension of the internal organization into the market has increased the control of the marketing process by subsidiaries. Internal controls can now be employed, for example through use of a strategy in which the input control of organizational culture is built up through salesmen being socialized into company values. The dual responsibility for customers shared by technicians and salesmen also forces conflicts into the open, creating information that facilitates control by management. This is seen as a way of creating a better balance between the forces of conflict and cooperation within the organization, there having been too much cooperation earlier. The balance between flexibility and continuity has also been improved, the loss in flexibility having been more than compensated for by the increase in profits through the increase in control and continuity.

The increase in internal control and in the resulting profits for *Wear and Tear* are interpreted in this book as being the result of a reduction in transaction costs through the creation of a greater balance between flexibility and rigidity, and also of better external control, inasmuch as distributors are more dependent upon the company than agents are. Switching costs are also greater for distributors, since it is more expensive for them to change suppliers. In addition, control of the whole marketing process including that of price has been improved, which is the most vital competitive tool on local markets. Harmony is treated, therefore, as being a major principle in marketing, for example in attempts to attain the right balance between the different products sold and also between different aspects of price. Pricing is controlled to a certain degree, but not particularly much, since flexibility in pricing is considered vital. Local management controls pricing by means of specific guidelines, although these allow salesmen a certain degree of freedom. Again, it is a question of finding the right balance between continuity and flexibility. The same principle is used internally in negotiating with other companies in the group regarding transfer prices. This means achieving the right balance between internal and external pricing, both from a local and a central perspective. The guidelines are also an expression of another important principle – that of the measurement of performance being the key to efficient control. In a more popular sense, this principle can be expressed as follows: if you cannot measure, you cannot control, and if you cannot control you cannot manage. For *Wear and Tear* this means reporting being an essential task for salesmen, although without this being made overly extensive, since most salesmen would consider this unnecessary work. Thus, a sensible trade-off needs to be made between needs of management to exert control and the willingness of subordinates to let themselves be controlled.

An important local issue regarding control that one should consider in *Wear and Tear*'s local sales organization concerns the risk of Chinese salesmen, in particular, leaving the company and taking customers with them. With the strong entrepreneurial spirit of many of the salesmen, they may well be thinking of opening up their own businesses. As a consequence, the turnover of salespeople in many industries is high. Chinese salesmen should not be given critical control of the customers of their own organization, therefore, since this creates an unbalanced situation involving dangers to the company. Such a situation can be rectified by increasing the control of the sales process, the responsibility for customers being distributed among persons in positions representing different functions, for example primary sales, technical support, and after sales, each category being allowed to develop customer relations of its own. Increased control is also achieved by process control, through letting the regional managing director participate actively in the marketing carried on within the various markets rather than isolating him at regional headquarters.

Figure 6.2 Wear and Tear'*s local organization*

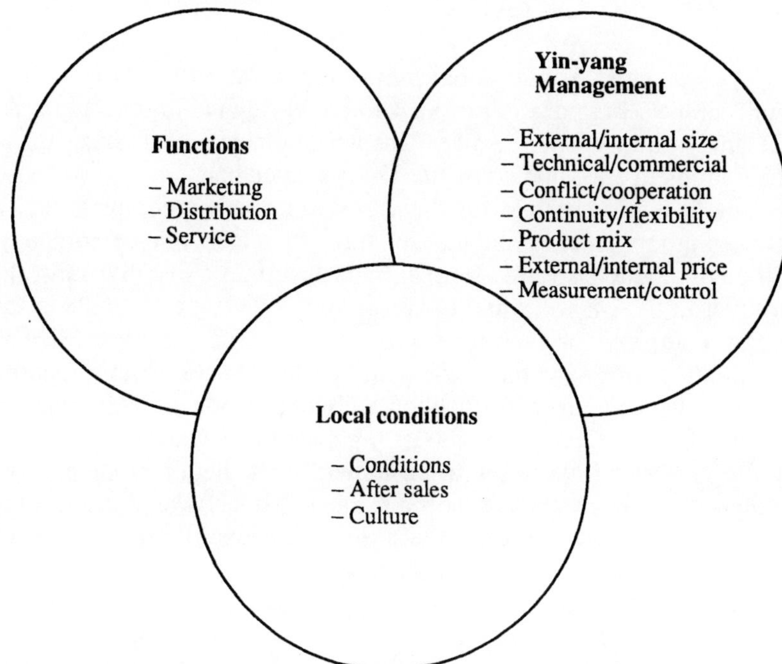

Wear and Tear's local organization is summarized schematically in Figure 6.2. This adaptation of management through use of the Yin-Yang principle is a nice example of how a local business culture can be used to further efficiency and market competitiveness, which indeed are among the ultimate principles subscribed to by West-European TNCs. The binary thinking expressed here in the ideas of balance and harmony can be seen as related to the idea of trade-off inherent in transaction cost theory. In the latter, different contrasting dimensions are balanced so that transaction costs are reduced. In this sense, the transaction cost principle is one-dimensional, the Yin-Yang principle, being of two-dimensional character. This difference is suggestive of the large institutional differences between Western market-oriented TNCs and the environment in SEA. Within *Wear and Tear*'s subsidiary in the region, these differences are reconciled by subordinating the

Yin-Yang principle to the transaction cost principle, since creating harmony within the organization in differing ways is not seen as an end in itself but as a means of increasing efficiency.

MATRIX ORGANIZATION

Weldprod, which has a global matrix organization, finds it hard to adapt its local organization in SEA to its worldwide organization. As was analysed in greater detail in Chapter 5, this is a general organizational problem encountered by the TNCs studied here.

Thus, it is not possible for *Weldprod* to achieve a complete match between group structure and the structure of the local market company. Although products are sold from each of the group's five divisions, the turnover in SEA is too small to allow there to be separate units in the market company for each main product type. The market in SEA is also different, for example in the major customers being more focused on manufacturing processes than on individual products. This suggests the need for a different type of sales organization, a matter also implied by the fact that linkages with customers work better in such small markets in which customers meet a single salesman who represents the whole company rather than their meeting several salesmen, each representing a different set of products.

It is thus not feasible to try to reproduce the global matrix organization of the company locally. Neither is it possible to completely adapt the organization to local premises. Compromises are therefore necessary. The compromise for *Weldprod* involves group structure, which it adapts to local conditions as much as possible. A similar compromise reached at *Pills*, as described above, is to place product specialists, which small market companies need for the sale of new or advanced products but cannot afford on their own, at a central location in the region. These specialists, who train salesmen and assist in selling, are paid by, and are normally organized within the product-oriented companies, but are placed in the regional unit.

The local organization may thus represent some kind of compromise between existing group structure and local conditions. A trade-off is often made, both as regards the vertical relation between global product interests and the interests of the local market, and between different vertical relations within the horizontal dimension. It is very much a question of establishing and maintaining an efficient mechanism for translating local demands into 'supplies' obtained from the group, for example within a matrix organization. However, it is mostly the other way around, particularly at an early stage of operations within SEA, priority being given instead to the product aspect in the matrix. This can result in the marketing strategy and the market organization in the local market being inefficient. The match between the two dimensions tends then to be poor, making the overall organization of the TNC in question inefficient.

Hence, for the demands of the matrix type organization to be fulfilled, it is critical that a 'coupling mechanism' be developed between the 'pipelines' coming from the product companies and the 'pipelines' coming from the market. Otherwise, there will be no efficient trade-off between global integration and local responsiveness. As has been shown in earlier chapters, an efficient market organization is critical for maintaining the competitive strength of the firm. The better marketing is organized, the more difficult it is for competitors to imitate.

ORGANIZATION OF MARKETING TO PROJECTS

As discussed above, small markets create problems when there is only an economic basis for there to be one market company to represent the group. One major problem found in the study concerns how the individual subsidiary should organize the diverse activities of selling products and selling to projects, particularly when the company is involved in large and complex multinational projects (Jansson, 1993). It is frustrating for a company involved in selling a project in its market if the main purchasing decisions are taken outside the company's area of responsibility by the main contractor or the financier of the project. In such a case, the subsidiary has very little control over its sales, since the company can only influence the project but not sell to it. Another difficult issue that can arise concerns how the costs and benefits of a project are to be shared when several subsidiaries of the group are involved. An individual company may make a large effort to sell to a project, yet the result may show up somewhere else in the group. Some groups have cross-border commissions which help the companies involved to negotiate sharing. The organization of multinational projects can also be troublesome for individual subsidiaries, which usually organize their resources for the more regular 'bread and butter' business of selling and distributing standard products. If subsidiaries become too dependent upon projects, the problems in reaching sales targets that are only open to doing business at intermittent periods of time may wreak havoc on the whole financial planning. It is therefore important that the product companies involved commit themselves to the activities of their subsidiaries and provide them with support. Marketing to projects is a long-term activity that requires close technical and commercial contacts between the respective units. A subsidiary may lack familiarity with many of the special aspects of a project. Much greater resources and stamina tend to be required to carry out projects than are needed for 'bread and butter' activities. Some groups have perfected their organization to meet such demands through forming special companies with appropriate customer specialist functions. They work as contractors, putting together projects for particular customer needs. Products for such projects are chiefly purchased (sub-contracted) from internal suppliers, although outside suppliers may also be involved. However, local demand, or even the regional demand in SEA or the whole of East Asia, may be insufficient for it to be practical for a group to establish separate market companies, subordinate to more specific 'project' companies, for marketing to projects. There may at most be a limited distribution of work within a group, the market company handling the marketing of small to medium-sized projects, and the 'project' or product company (both products and projects may be sold) handling the marketing of large projects. The highest form of specialization is to be found among subsidiaries that have built up an additional capability of their own for selling to certain types of projects, for example subsidiaries that serve as regional technical centres and also have regional responsibility for such activities.

On the whole, organizing the sale to projects and preparing for business of this type is difficult for a group. The group has to mobilize a task force and pool its resources when an opportunity turns up. If the marketing to a project is not co-ordinated for the group as a whole, the customer can play the individual companies in the group off against each other. This can have a detrimental effect on the group as a whole. Main contractors, for example, usually have purchase offices in many parts of the world. If each office were to ask for a price quotation from the subsidiary located in its area, the prices would usually differ due to variations in local conditions. Obviously, coordination in marketing is called for.

The size of the TNC has a decisive influence on the effectiveness of its project organization. Too small a company cannot handle large multinational projects at all, since there must be a central unit for coordinating purposes. However, a huge multinational organization may also be inefficient, since its organization may be too sluggish, having long communication channels and be slow in making all the necessary contacts. A smaller and more flexible organization may more easily pool resources and concentrate them intensively during a short span of time.

REGIONAL ORGANIZATION

Most of the TNCs studied have some kind of regional organization in SEA. The regional functions involved can include administration, marketing, manufacturing, purchasing, finance, and various types of support (Jansson, 1991).

One of *Telecom*'s areas of business in SEA started to expand rapidly from the mid-1980s on, and six joint venture companies and one agent were soon operating in the area. The success here resulted in a conflict between the product division and one of the local organizations regarding the organizing of a project. Since the capacity for managing the project was lacking locally, the project was organized by the product division and was managed by people new to the region who were sent there from Europe. One of the regional representatives, who had made a major contribution in selling the project and who had had most of the customer contacts was pushed aside. This led to a serious conflict with the customer representatives, who preferred dealing with people they knew.

A regional office was established to solve problems such as these. It had the following tasks:

1. Development of sophisticated software systems tailormade to assist local customers in the areas of planning, implementation and operations.
2. Assistance to other *Telecom* subsidiaries and to associated companies within the areas of engineering, project management and computer software development.
3. Market coordination within the Far East region.

This office has full responsibility for the region. The local subsidiaries and the various associated companies report to this office rather than to the product division management in Europe.

The establishment of a regional organization increases both national responsiveness and the coordination on a regional basis of adaptations made to the different countries' environments. By developing strategies special to the region and having qualified persons implementing them, customer demands could be met more effectively, for example demands requiring local presence and continuous contacts together with quick responses to questions, where delays caused by long-distance contacts with Europe were not accepted. A regional organization functioning in this way reduces both marketing and administrative distance, acting as an intelligence unit for the product division as well as for other group units through being well informed regarding political, economic and technological developments in the region. Keeping costs for well educated personnel low is an important factor in the decision of where to place such an office, the ready availability of such persons improving recruitment possibilities.

After having left the establishment period behind, the main goals for this regional office are to cement and improve the company's permanent presence in the region, to develop new markets, and to improve project organization performance. The establishment of a regional office in this case has been highly successful and has led to an expansion of the office's geographic responsibility so as to encompass the whole of South and East Asia (Bernhardsson and Lindner, 1991).

Most of the TNCs studied are sales companies. There are three main sales and marketing functions that were found at the regional level:

1. To control and coordinate sales in the region and also to serve that function either directly or indirectly in those countries, in which the TNC is without representation by sales companies.
2. To participate in marketing and market intelligence activities.
3. To provide the market companies with marketing support.

This largely coincides with what was found in an earlier study of the regional organization of TNCs in Latin America and in Europe as well as in Asia (Grosse, 1982).

A critical organizational issue for technologically advanced TNCs concerns how to organize in local markets the connection between basic R. & D., product development and customer needs. Although many of the TNCs that were studied have technical expertise in the region this is largely expertise that has been brought there to assist in the marketing of technologically complex products. The little engineering expertise established is found at the regional level, mainly to serve customer specialists in adapting or developing products to satisfy local needs.

Another major regional marketing function, one concerned with the selling of projects to governments, involves the building up of local contact nets with high government officials and participating in various stages of negotiation. The country manager of the local subsidiary is often considered to have too low an authority for such large business deals.

Both formal and informal regional cooperation is important. Possibilities for controlling local activities from a regional office located in the area are better than those for doing so from a European office. Decisions are also improved through such regionally-based control, due to the shorter communication channels involved, which yield quicker response to market demands and facilitate the starting of new local business ventures through knowledge and authority being localized to the area. This is an important aspect of the fast growing Southeast Asian markets.

Five types of regional organization are found:

1. A separate regional company that controls the market companies there.
2. A separate regional administrative office with a managing director for the region.
3. Regional functions, either organized within one of the market companies for all of the market companies together or spread out among them.
4. A single regional company that in a very natural way has responsibility for the entire region.
5. Regional functions being organized from the home base.

Through a regional organization, local interests within the group are supported. This is illustrated in the next section of this chapter in connection with transfer pricing. A regional company that negotiates for all the subsidiaries has greater bargaining power than individual subsidiaries that negotiate for themselves. The various types of regional organization listed above are presented there in descending order of strength, from the strongest form to the weakest. The first two forms are typical of large TNCs with several market companies in the region, each representing several product companies. Through regional presence, local interest can be given particular weight in dealings with the product companies. With the establishment of a regional company, a mini-group is formed within the region, one which is on a parity with the product companies in the overall organization of the group. This is a two-dimensional organization, but one without a formal matrix. Any given market company within the group is assigned to one of two possible types, either a regional company or a product company. Business between regional and product companies is governed more by prices than by authority. Like a matrix organization, such an organization is characterized by low information and enforcement costs, and by high bargaining costs. As discussed earlier, pricing strategy plays a critical role in influencing these various costs.

The presence of a regional administrative office tends by comparison to involve a certain weakening of the representation of local interests. Having regional functions within a global product organization puts the organization thus created in an intermediate position between the product and market companies, particularly in SEA, where the local subsidiaries are more independent than their European counterparts. In the two remaining, more advisory types of organization there is still greater likelihood than in the type just mentioned for regional functions to be only loosely organized.

As discussed in Chapter 4, the geographical organization takes form gradually and is institutionalized when the regional activities reach a certain momentum. Later, when the regional activities have become stabilized, it sometimes disappears or is changed into a more decentralized form. *Pacmat*'s regional organization, for instance, has gradually been decentralized and more or less abolished. In 1991, very few of its regional functions remained. On the whole, however, some kind of regional organization, however limited it may be in scope, was found to be common among the TNCs that were studied.

ORGANIZATION OF TRANSFER PRICING

As observed in Chapter 3, a transfer price system is one of the main controls of a TNC. However, since groups design their systems differently, the constraints on the pricing adopted by individual companies vary. Some pricing systems of the groups that were studied allowed individual companies to influence transfer prices, whereas others did not. Transfer prices were in any case constructed internally.[1]

In TNCs generally, transfer price bargaining sometimes take place between separate units, whereas internal prices are sometimes fixed by a central unit, which publishes price lists to be adhered to by the individual units, coordination being achieved by this central administration of transfer prices. Individual units are chiefly controlled by general directives, of which transfer prices are only one aspect. Although this is the opposite of market governance, since transfer prices are not determined by market forces, the situation of the individual company is similar to that for market governance, in that the prices cannot be influenced by an individual unit, since once decided upon, must be followed. This latter, centralized form of price regime was not observed in any of the TNCs examined in the present study.

Internal pricing differs from market pricing in the prices being controlled partly by factors of the market, and partly by bilateral and trilateral governance, as well as by authority. How these factors are combined is determined in part by the transaction costs involved.[2]

This section illustrates the fact that conflict between local market interests and global product interests within a TNC is reflected in pricing. Thus, pricing can be seen as a mediator between such major interests within the group's organization, transaction costs being important in determining the outcome.

Transfer Pricing Policies

Eccles (1985) makes the distinction between three basic transfer pricing policies: mandated full cost, mandated market-based and exchange autonomy. In the first of these, the group decides on the transfer price being the same as the full cost of the product, it thus having only a limited role in resource allocation. Price under such circumstances is not market-based at all, since internal transactions cannot be replaced by external transactions. However, bargaining costs may also be incurred due to conflicts regarding how to measure costs and how to account for discrepancies between standard costs and actual costs.

In mandated market-based transfers, profits are added, these being supposed to reflect market opportunities. The main drawback with this price regime is that it may lead to expensive products, since they are 'marked up twice'. An internal buyer may thus buy fewer products. Mandated market transfers can be determined both by authority and by external factors, prices to some extent reflecting an efficient allocation of resources. The policy expressed in this way is based on a comparison with outside transactions. The role of the price varies with the external governance form and the type of product involved. If internal pricing is modelled in terms of an external market situation characterized by bilateral governance, pricing will be cost-based. If, on the other hand, trilateral governance is the basis of comparison, transfer pricing is mainly characterized by competitive bidding. Price can also work as an information generator, particularly when conflicts become a basic ingredient of relations between internal units. This is emphasized by Eccles and White (1988, pp. 38-9.)

> In the multidivisional firm, the role of prices is different from that described in standard economic theory, where prices form information consolidators that ensure efficient resource allocation. Although economists have argued that transfer prices can play a similar role in the multidivisional firm, in fact their major role is to be information generators. Information is produced through conflict and contributes to the ability of top management to control lower levels both directly and indirectly.

This quotation illustrates the relation between information and bargaining costs for a transfer price policy of this sort.

In exchange autonomy transfers, internal suppliers can be replaced by external suppliers. This is the most market-like situation, one mostly applying to standard products. Price plays a role here similar to its role in economic theory, since it determines how resources are allocated. Authority is of minor importance under such circumstances.

Price discretion among the market companies in SEA that were studied depends on how the group is organized. A global product organization appears to allow little freedom, since in such an organization a product company has a worldwide responsibility for its products. Subsidiaries are divided up among the product companies and are subordinated to them. Much of the authority regarding marketing rests with the divisions thus formed. However, the study also shows that for certain parts of the organization, specifically small market companies, price discretion tends to be greater. In the more traditional multinational organization of a TNC, for example in the mother-daughter type organization, subsidiaries are more independent, possessing a greater freedom of its individual units than in a global product organization, the central unit not interfering as long as parties stay within the guidelines determined for the group. For exchange autonomy transfers and mandated market-based transfers, the pricing behaviour here to some extent resembles the external pricing found within the bilateral governance form.

Mandated market-based policy

For the TNCs that were studied, most of the internal transfers were either reflective of mandated full-cost or of mandated market-based pricing policies, in these a very vital constraint price discretion being the cost accounting system of the group, which specifies the rules for how costs are calculated and on which costs prices are to be based.

These rules are common for the entire group and are seldom changed, constituting the most important basis for the whole planning and budget system. All the industrial groups that were studied practised, particularly at the beginning of their activities in SEA, a product-focused absorption approach to pricing, which very much restricts the possibilities for market companies to adapt prices to local conditions. This is a major factor behind the emphasis on product quality in the competitive strategies pursued by these companies (Jansson, 1993).

As expected, local units within a global product organization were found to have little influence on internal prices, which were often fixed from 'above' by the product divisions. This was most obvious in cases in which standard products were being sold, the subsidiaries were small, and these were located in countries far removed from the home offices. More unexpectedly it was found that the specific local market conditions in SEA rarely led to the group giving special price concessions to local units. Transfer pricing within a global product organization is illustrated by the *Food equipment* case, certain complementary aspects of this being described in the cases of *Weldprod*, *Paving systems* and *Wear and Tear*.

When there is an element of mother-daughter organization within the global product organization, as in the case of *Conmine*, there seem both to be greater price negotiations and a greater degree of local impact on transfer prices. The highest degree of local autonomy in transfer pricing of any of the TNCs studied is found in the *Tooltec* case, in which prices represent the major means of control of the business occurring between the main parts of the organization, namely the product divisions and the regional divisions.

Fixed transfer prices

Food equipment has a regional unit in Singapore that coordinates the activities of the market companies in the region. The links between these companies and the product companies pass through this unit. Because of its central location in the 'pipelines' between market and product companies, it works as a kind of 'linking pin'. The organization of the market companies is such that these are divided up among different product companies.

The responsibility for budgeting and for deciding on transfer prices rests with the product companies. The cost accounting system is based on absorption costing, the full manufacturing cost representing a price norm (informal) below which products cannot be sold. Another norm employed is to have non-negotiable fixed-transfer prices, at least for components (standard products), so as to avoid internal trade and the ensuing bargaining process. However, the flexible margins found do allow negotiations to take place to some degree, since certain engineering costs and other developmental costs are included in the transfer prices. Still, it is mainly fixed-priced components which are bought, these being purchased directly from factories. This facilitates a comparison of internal prices with outside prices, and reduces the role of authority.

All transfer prices within the group are revised annually, exceptions to this rule occurring only when the outside prices rise sharply. Since it is hard to pass on such a price increase to local customers, a permanent or delayed price rise is either negotiated with the product company under such circumstances or the local margins are reduced.

A very similar pattern for the organization of the transfer price system, the setting of customer prices, and for pricing behaviour is evident in another TNC (*Weldprod*), which has a matrix organization involving product divisions. However, since its turnover in the region is less than *Food equipment*'s and its organization is smaller, with fewer market companies, the need for regional coordination in the company is low. The SEA region is managed from Singapore, cooperation with the market company in Malaysia being close.

Another large TNC with a global product organization, *Paving systems,* used to have only a small sales subsidiary for the entire region and for several other parts of Asia, one located in Singapore. This subsidiary was a largely independent company that operated on a commission basis and could be likened to a kind of agent that acted as an intermediary between the group, on the one hand, and customers in the region, on the other. Since the subsidiary in question specialized in only one industry, it represented only a small fraction of the group's products, which otherwise were sold through local agents.

The market conditions with which *Paving systems* is faced are similar in many ways to those of the other companies considered in this chapter, for example in having low and stable prices, together with customers that haggle and are price conscious. However, the company is in a new market for the region, one in which there is practically no local competition. At the same time, customers are at least partly aware of there being competing products that can be imported from other parts of the world.

Transfer prices of the company were originally determined both by the product division and by the market. One type of major equipment was purchased in accordance with an internal price list. Due to conditions such as these, relations both with the group and with customers tended to be very market-like, it being up to each subsidiary to decide which products of the group were profitable to sell in the region in question. Absorption costing was practised, the bottom-line for a subsidiary needing to cover the full costs and earn a profit. The group did not interfere with a subsidiary's external pricing. However, this situation began to change in 1991 in connection with a reorganization of the product division in Europe which was the supplier, many more products being added then through a merger. A major change that this involved for the subsidiary was that the coordination of the joint external pricing became more differentiated.

Another small subsidiary company, which represents *Wear and Tear*, has the whole region as its area of activity. It operates under conditions very similar to those under which *Paving systems* did earlier. Certain major differences for this company compared with the latter is that it belongs to a much smaller TNC, that is not divisionalized, and that it can be classified as belonging to a mother-daughter organization. The TNC in question has a very narrow product range, making it possible for the subsidiary to represent the entire group in the region. Like *Paving systems*' subsidiary described above, it is very independent. It obtains a 15% commission on its sales, just as an agent would. Internal prices are fixed and there is no dialogue with the parent company regarding pricing. In much the same way, prices towards agents in the region are also more or less fixed. In other respects, the company operates under market conditions similar to those of the other companies considered above, employing a competitive strategy that plays down price. It also encounters fierce Japanese competition on its various markets.

Negotiated transfer prices

When prices are negotiated between the market companies in SEA and the product companies in Europe that are suppliers, this usually takes place within the framework of an absorption-cost system. Such TNCs are characterized as having a mandated market-based transfer policy. *Conmine*, for example, has a global product organization, but such that the local units in SEA are related to the group in a manner that more resembles a mother-daughter organization. For this TNC, internal prices within SEA are based on feedback from the markets which function in the following way: the prices are proposed by the market companies on the basis of the local market conditions, their proposals being communicated to the product company in Europe, which decides on the price. However, since the product company considers this information to often be biased, it sends its own people to SEA to investigate the markets in order to independently obtain a more adequate basis for its decisions, particularly in cases in which special prices are requested by the Asian subsidiaries. There is no joint pricing in relation to the customer by the two companies. Rather, pricing comes about indirectly through the bargaining that is carried on regarding transfer prices. The additional information the product company needs is mainly obtained by visiting the market companies. However, as one managing director pointed out, the effectiveness of such efforts can be questioned, since they also allow the market company and its managing director to control the information provided thus serving the ends of the market company. Such behaviour was more common before 1986, however, and was a result of the organization found in those days, each unit which tended to maximize its own profit, which was reported directly to group management and was not consolidated in the product divisions. Pricing then was more opportunistic, which led to a strong interest in the control of internal pricing.

Since an organizational change which was carried out in 1986, the occurrence and effects of such behaviour have been reduced, the product company now supplying many market companies within the group directly. Prices are compared and the prices consolidated for the whole group. Furthermore, the transfer prices employed are normally ones used in common for all of the TNCs' market companies in SEA. The products are all distributed through Singapore, the location most economical for stocking products due to the country's free trade zone status. Thus, the transfer prices in particular, and customer prices to a certain extent, of the different market companies tend to be coordinated with each other. As one of the managing directors suggested, such a system leads to considerable dialogue occurring between the market and product companies, at the same time as the weighing of local interests against group interests is viewed as necessary and positive. There is more long-term thinking today than there was earlier, when the accounting system only indicated the individual profitability of each of the companies. Common group interests are taken into consideration much more now and competition between the market companies has been reduced.

Price support to the market companies was more common during the establishment period. Today, internal price levels for some products are fixed, while they vary for others, for example when competition makes it impossible to keep 'ordinary' price levels or where a special price is requested for a large order. Because of the very competitive nature of the markets generally, it even happens that a market company requests being able to buy at a price below the full costs to the manufacturing company, particularly when a product is introduced in a local market. During the first years, there was more of a mandated full-cost policy, where manufacturing-oriented costs were simply passed on to the next stage. With the growing market-orientation, complexity has increased, making it necessary for the parties to learn more about each other's problems and to bargain more. A contribution approach to pricing tends to be utilized in the very competitive markets here.

An important reason for reducing transfer prices in many cases may be to allow the local company to either achieve a certain minimum profit or reduce profits for tax reasons. However, such considerations are seen generally as confusing pricing, rendering it more difficult to reach 'maximum' price levels for the group as a whole, as well as obstructing efficiency evaluation of the various units. Such 'window dressing' or purely financial motives for manipulating transfer prices are rare within the group, just as it is for the TNCs generally that were studied.

All in all, transfer prices to the region are lower than for products sold in the European markets. The prices agreed upon by the parties are normally fixed either for six months or for a year, and changes are only allowed when the input prices rise sharply. When internal prices are changed, the market companies usually try to revise their prices to customers. However, this is not as easy and automatic as the revision of transfer prices, partly because prices cannot be changed during the period when an offer (tender) is valid. One way to solve this problem is to include price clauses in the contract which allow price increases to be made in response to changes in exchange rates.

Exchange autonomy

Internal pricing in one of the TNCs studied, namely *Tooltec*, follows a pattern reminiscent of exchange autonomy. There is a clear demarcation between the company's global product organization for its main markets and its regional organization for its minor markets. There is considerable freedom in bargaining about price between these major internal units. Market control seems to largely replace hierarchical control in the small market companies of the group which are located in countries far from the home office. Compared with the TNCs examined heretofore, *Tooltec* has a stronger geographical emphasis within its organization, involving a closer coordination of the market companies within a regional organization, making product companies and regional companies more equal partners in negotiations. The group's market companies within SEA are less strongly connected with its product companies than those of *Food equipment*'s were shown to be. Thus its component companies in the region have a high degree of autonomy of exchange.

Originally, *Tooltec*'s accounting system was based entirely on absorption costing, its market companies in the region adding costs of their own and a reasonable profit to the internal prices charged by the regional company. However, when a change in group organization was introduced, there was a gradual move away from such a cost-plus system to a negotiated transfer price system instead, something which is more typical of an exchange autonomy.

The company's transfer prices (to the region) are based partly on the basic cost of the products and partly on the local market situation. Thus, the product companies tend to adapt their prices somewhat to local conditions. In exceptional cases, for example when new products are introduced, the product companies even agree to reduce their prices to a level below the full cost of the product. Price negotiations are usually tough within the group, profit thinking being pronounced at all levels. This favours self-seeking price behaviour. The regional company, in its negotiations with the product companies, where it represents all the market companies in the region, is not much interested in the size of the profits the product companies earn, and at the same time the product companies do not care much what profits the regional group of companies earns as long as they make profits themselves. Some of the product companies send people of their own to SEA to visit both customers and middlemen so as to obtain better insight into the price situation there.

Tooltec's pricing process is characterized by negotiated bidding, involving individual profit thinking being built into the organization in such a way that a high degree of exchange autonomy is created. The profits of the market companies are consolidated and kept within the region, and are simply reported to the parent company rather than being divided among the product companies.

In contrast, *Tooltec*'s considerably larger market companies located in Europe and in North America are consolidated with the product companies that belong to it. A consequence of this is that the degree of independence of individual companies within the group varies, being greatest for the regional companies and for the product companies. In negotiations between these major units, the product companies attend to their global market interests and are not prepared to give special favours to the regional company in SEA. This makes it impossible to 'optimize' the local market shares by any marked reduction in transfer prices. Local recessions, for example, which result in a lowering of customer prices there, must mainly be absorbed and dealt with locally, since possibilities for passing on the effects of the lower prices to the rest of the group are limited. At the same time, the absorption potential of the small individual market companies in price-competitive local markets tends to be low and for the product companies they represent only small customers. Through being united, however, in the region as a whole in their approach to the product companies, their combined absorption potential is emphasized and their bargaining power is increased considerably. This is an important reason for there being a regional company to coordinate local activities.

The bargaining process and the tough price negotiations just described can be seen as representing the characteristics of a two-dimensional organization with two strong parties that oppose each other, creating a marked conflict between the local/regional interests and the global product interests. Earlier, *Tooltec* exercised a certain degree of management of the transfer prices with the aim of an apportioning of profits and taxes between the different companies. However, this was abandoned since it confused management too much, contradicting in many ways the control system the group employed, which is based on market control of the individual units. The financial management of transfer prices is also inappropriate to a two-dimensional organization, in which it is important that one achieves an efficient trade-off between global integration and local responsiveness.

Regional transfer price

Tooltec coordinates pricing within the region through a transfer price system. The price strategy this represents, in contrast to exchange between the region and the group outside SEA, represents mandated market-based pricing. This involves the regional company deciding on the prices to be employed in transactions between itself and the market companies, a rather sensitive issue. Since a high degree of decentralization is found in the organization of the overall group, the costs and prices of the market companies cannot be controlled very stringently so as to not violate the balance between control and incentives. Thus, the coordination of prices aims mainly at creating a basis for deciding on the transfer price to be used in transactions with the product companies, the local market companies being responsible for customer prices. The internal control of a highly complex regional price system such as this can be improved by the development of a regional management information system employing a customer- and middleman-oriented accounting. Hopefully, the development of such a system will make it possible to equalize internal prices somewhat between the different market companies. This is difficult in a region in which each market is more or less unique, in which in certain countries there is a flow of products from low to high price segments, and in which the markets of different countries are interconnected, for example through the smuggling of products from low-duty to high-duty countries.

CONCLUSIONS

In order to clarify the local organization of the 17 TNCs from the (in European eyes) distant Southeast Asian markets studied here, traditional theories of the multinational firm based on transaction costs were expanded to include more organizational aspects. The result is a theory of hierarchical multinationalism.

Such a theory of the organizational economics of TNCs provides an explanation of why internal organization seems in most cases to be the most efficient type of governance form. First, local internal organization based on a high degree of local responsiveness seems to be efficient as such. Second, local transactions, mostly organized as bilateral and trilateral governance, are usually effective for internalization in a transnational organization. These factors are reinforced by the impact of non-economic institutions such as culture and the legal system as seen for example in the low degree of protection provided for property rights in SEA. However, as was analysed above for the *Weldprod* case and which was discussed more extensively in Chapter 5, there are instances in which local organization in SEA does not seem to be linked in an effective way with a TNC's global organization.

As was likewise illustrated by *Weldprod*, and was analysed in greater detail in Chapter 5, local organization is usually a compromise between existing group structure and local conditions. A complete reproduction of the global organization would be inefficient in small markets because of high establishment costs. The need for a high degree of adaptability to the specific circumstances found in these markets creates a strong conflict between global product interests and local interests. This results in inefficiencies, mainly through bargaining costs being high. Such problems are hard to solve due to the marginal importance of local business to the concern as a whole.

Organizational efficiency can be increased by supporting local interests through actions taken by the regional organization. Transaction costs can be reduced by having such activities as those of management and marketing located at the regional level rather than at the global level. Different types of regional organization give differing weight to local interests. In a global product organization, the stronger a role the local/regional interests play, the more a two-dimensional form the organization assumes. This generally results in an increase in bargaining costs, but this is more than counterbalanced by the reduction in information and enforcement costs which results.

The type of group organization that is found affects transfer pricing behaviour, involving as it does the question of how much price negotiation is permitted, bargaining being least in various market-based transfers. Even if such internal transactions have certain qualities of market governance, mostly due to the products exchanged being standard ones, these internal transactions are not part of this external governance form, since they cannot be replaced by outside transactions. The degree of decentralization found in global organization also influences internal pricing behaviour. The greater freedom of some subsidiaries, for example, makes the transfers in which they are involved more market-like. This is particularly true for the smaller market companies belonging to various of the smaller TNCs. Although there is no total freedom to replace internal parties with external parties here, transfer pricing under such conditions can nevertheless be considered to involve exchange autonomy. This also demonstrates the fact that parity in price negotiations necessitates efficient regional coordination.

Another conclusion to be drawn is that trust in the local subsidiary saves internal transaction costs both by limiting information search and by reconciling global and local interests. However, if information is biased due to the opportunism of the market company, transaction costs are not reduced, since there is a risk that the separate investigations of the market there do not result in better decisions. Decisions there might even be inferior compared with getting information through the usual channels.

The relationship between trust and transaction costs is complex. Strong trust may make the parties complacent. If it is too easy to get a low price from an internal supplier, the market company may not try hard enough to obtain good prices from customers. This can lower the profit for the group as a whole (group interests). It is thus important that the transfer prices proposed be well motivated and that the other party can evaluate them correctly. This is particularly true if the market company wishes to reduce the price below that which would cover the full costs to the product company.

There is a limit to how high transaction costs and bureaucratic costs should be in contacts between group units. If they become too high, internal organization becomes inefficient and an external organization more favourable, for example in contracting with a distributor. No such cases were found, however, among the TNCs that were studied. Rather, as was illustrated for *Tooltec*, an own representation in the local market can be more efficient due to improvement in the market information and in the control of prices. Growth is faster and the approach to marketing is more long-term. Business in SEA is still growing rapidly and has in most cases not yet reached the point where transaction costs begin to increase due to the efficiency of internal organization. There are also cases in which this steep increase in local activity has led to inefficiency for the group as a whole, paving the way for a complete reorganization of the TNC. Management of transfer prices was uncommon among the TNCs studied, chiefly because of the adverse effects it has on efficient control of a TNC.

NOTES

1. An excellent review of research on transfer pricing is found in Eccles and White (1988, p. 21).
2. A combination of price and authority in the allocation of resources is utilized by socialist economies and by firms in socialist countries (see Eccles and White (1988, p. 18) for research on this issue).

Bibliography

Alchian, A.A. and Demsetz, H. (1972), 'Production, Information Costs and Economic Organization', *American Economic Review*, 62, pp. 777-95.

Alchian, A.A. and Woodward, S. (1988), 'The Firm is Dead; Long Live the Firm. A Review of Oliver E. Williamson's The Economic Institutions of Capitalism', *Journal of Economic Literature*, XXVI, March, pp. 65-79.

Aldrich, H.E. (1979), *Organizations and Environment*, Englewood Cliffs, N.J: Prentice Hall.

Anderson, E. and Weitz, B.A. (1983), 'Make or Buy Decisions: A Framework for Analyzing Vertical Integration Issues in Marketing', Working Paper No. 83-001R, The Wharton School, University of Pennsylvania, Philadelphia.

Anderson, E. and Gatignon, H. (1986), 'Modes of Foreign Entry: A Transaction Cost Analysis and Propositions', *Journal of International Business Studies*, Fall, pp. 1-26.

Aoki, A. and Tachiki, D.S. (1992), 'Overseas Japanese Business Operations: The Emerging Role of Regional Headquarters', *Pacific Business and Industries*, 1, pp. 28-39.

Armour, H.O. and Teece, D.J. (1978), 'Organization Structure and Economic Performance: A Test of the Multidivisional Hypothesis', *Bell Journal of Economics*, 9, pp. 106-22.

Assarsson, B. (1989), 'Prissättning i den svenska tillverkningsindustrin: en empirisk undersökning', in P-O. Bjuggren and G. Skogh (eds), *Företaget – en kontraktsekonomisk analys*, Stockholm: SNS, pp. 159-75.

Bain, J.S. (1956), *Barriers to New Competition*, Cambridge, Mass: Harvard University Press.

Barney, J.B. and Ouchi, W.G. (1986), *Organizational Economics. Towards a New Paradigm for Understanding and Studying Organizations*, San Francisco, Cal: Jossey-Bass.

Bartlett, C. (1986), 'Building and Managing the Transnational: The New Organizational Challenge', in M. Porter (ed.), *Competition in Global Industries*, Boston, Mass.: Harvard Business School Press, pp. 367-401.

Bartlett, C., Y. Doz and G. Hedlund (eds) (1990), *Managing the Global Firm*, London/New York: Routledge.

Bartlett, C. and Ghoshal, S. (1989), *Managing Across Borders: The Transnational Solution*, Boston, Mass.: The Free Press.

Bartlett, C. and Ghoshal, S. (1991), 'Building Transnational Capabilities: The Management Challenge', INSEAD Working Paper No. 91/43/SM.

Behrman, J. and Grosse, R. (1990), *International Business and Governments. Issues and Institutions*, South Carolina: University of South Carolina Press.

Bernhardsson, A. and Lindner, P. (1991), 'Marketing and Organization. A Descriptive Case Study', Thesis, Örebro University.

Blau, P. (1964), *Exchange and Power in Social Life*, New York: Wiley.

Blau, P. (1968), 'The Hierarchy of Authority in Organizations', *American Journal of Sociology*, 73, pp. 453-67.

Blau, P. (1987), 'Microprocess and Macrostructure', in K.S. Cook, (ed.), *Social Exchange Theory*, Beverly Hills, Cal.: Sage, pp. 83-100.

Bond, M.H. (ed.) (1986), *The Psychology of the Chinese People*, Hong Kong: Oxford University Press.

Borg, M. (1987), *International Transfers of Managers in Multinational Corporations. Transfer Patterns and Organizational Control,* Acta Universitatis Upsaliensis, Studia Oeconomiae Negotiorum 27, Uppsala (dissertation).

Brunsson, N. (1982), 'Företagsekonomi – Avbildning eller Språkbildning', in N. Brunsson (ed.) *Företagsekonomi – sanning eller moral*, Lund: Studentlitteratur, pp. 100-12.

Buckley, P.J. (1987), *The Theory of the Multinational Enterprise*, Acta Universitatis Upsaliensis, Studia Oeconomiae Negotiorum 26, Uppsala.

Buckley, P.J. (1988a), 'The Limits of Explanation: Testing the Internalization Theory of the Multinational Enterprise', *Journal of International Business Studies*, 19, No. 2, pp. 181-93.

Buckley, P.J. (1988b), 'Organizational Forms and Multinational Companies', in S. Thompson and M. Wright (eds), *Internal Organization, Efficiency and Profit*, Oxford: Philip Allan Publishers, pp. 127-44.

Buckley, P.J. and Casson, M.C. (1976), *The Future of the Multinational Enterprise*, London: Macmillan.

Bulcke, D. van den (1984), 'Regional Headquarters and Employment

Decision Making. Belgian Evidence and European Relevance', paper, EIBA Conference, Rotterdam, 16-19 December.

Bulmer, M. (1979), 'Concepts in the Analysis of Qualitative Data', *Sociological Review*, 27, No. 4, pp. 651-77.

Butler, R. and Carney, M.G. (1983), 'Managing Markets: Implications for the Make-Buy Decision', *Journal of Management Studies*, 20, pp. 213-31.

Cable, J.R. (1988), 'Organizational Form and Economic Performance', in S. Thompson and M. Wright (eds), *Internal Organization, Efficiency and Profit*, Oxford: Philip Allan Publishers, pp. 12-37.

Calvet, A.L. (1980), *Markets and Hierarchies: Toward a Theory of International Business*, Massachusetts Institute of Technology (dissertation), Boston.

Calvet, A.L. (1981), 'A Synthesis of Foreign Direct Investment Theories and Theories of the Multinational Firm', *Journal of International Business Studies*, Vol. 12, pp. 43-59.

Calvet, A.L. and Naim, A. (1981), 'The Multinational Firm in Less Developed Countries: A Markets and Hierarchies Approach', paper, Joint EIBA/AIB Meeting, Barcelona, December 17-19.

Casson, M.C. (1985), 'Multinational Monopolies and International Cartels', in P.J. Buckley and M.C. Casson (eds), *The Economic Theory of the Multinational Enterprise: Selected Papers*, London: Macmillan, pp. 60-97.

Casson, M.C. (1987), *The Firm and the Market. Studies on Multinational Enterprise and the Scope of the Firm*. Oxford: Blackwell.

Caves, R.E. (1979), 'Industrial Organization, Corporate Strategy and Structure', *Journal of Economic Literature*, XVIII, March, pp. 64-92.

Caves, R.E. (1982), *Multinational Enterprise and Economic Analysis*, Cambridge: Cambridge University Press.

Chandler, A. (1962), *Strategy and Structure. Chapters in the History of the Industrial Enterprise*, Cambridge, Mass.: MIT Press.

Chandler, A. and H. Daems (eds) (1980), *Managerial Hierarchies. Comparative Perspectives on the Rise of the Modern Industrial Enterprise*, Cambridge, Mass: Harvard University Press.

Cheung, S.N.S. (1983), 'The Contractual Nature of the Firm', *Journal of Law and Economics*, 26, pp. 1-21.

Coase, R.H. (1937), 'The Nature of the Firm', *Economica*, 4, pp. 386-405.

Collin, S. (1990), *Aktiebolagets kontroll. Ett transaktionskostnadsteoretiskt inlägg i debatten om ägande och kontroll av aktiebolag och storföretag*, Lund (dissertation).

Cray, D. (1984), 'Control and Coordination in Multinational Corporations', *Journal of International Business Studies*, XV, No. 2, pp. 85-98.

Daems, H. (1980), 'Determinants of the Hierarchical Organization of Industry', working paper, European Institute for Advanced Studies in Management, Brussels.

Dahlman, A. and Fredriksson, E. (1989), 'The Car Industry of Malaysia Purchasing Strategies and Supplier Networks', master thesis, Department of Business Administration, School of Economics and Management, Lund University.

Davidson, W.H. and McFetridge, D.G. (1985), 'Key Characteristics in the Choice of International Technology Transfer Mode', *Journal of International Business Studies*, XVI, pp. 5-21.

Doz, Y. (1986), *Strategic Management in Multinational Companies*, Oxford: Pergamon.

Dugger, W.M. (1983), 'The Transaction Cost Analysis of Oliver E. Williamson: A New Synthesis', *Journal of Economic Issues*, Vol. 17, No. 1, pp. 95-114.

Dunning, J.H. (1981), *International Production and the Multinational Enterprise*, London: Allen & Unwin.

Dunning, J.H. (ed.) (1985), *Multinational Enterprises, Economic Structure and International Competitiveness*, Chichester: Wiley.

Dunning, J.H. (1988a), *Explaining International Production*, London: Allen & Unwin.

Dunning, J.H. (1988b), 'The Eclectic Paradigm of International Production: A Restatement and Some Possible Extensions', *Journal of International Business Studies*, Spring, pp. 1-31.

Dunning, J.H. and Rugman, A.T. (1983), 'The Influence of Hymer's Dissertation on the Theory of Foreign Direct Investment', *The American Economic Review*, 75, pp. 228-32.

Eccles, R.G. (1985), *The Transfer Pricing Problem. A Theory for Practice*, Lexington, Mass.: Lexington Books.

Eccles, R.G. and White, H.C. (1987), 'Firm and Market Interfaces of Profit Center Control', in S. Lindenberg, J. S. Coleman and S. Nowak (eds), *Approaches to Social Theory*, New York: Russel Sage, pp. 203-220.

Eccles, R.G. and White, H.C. (1988), 'Price and Authority in Inter-Profit Center Transactions', *American Journal of Sociology*, 94, Supplement, pp. 17-51.

Edgren, J., Rhenman, E., and Skärvad, P.M. (1983), *Divisionalise-*

ring och därefter, Stockholm: Management Media.

Egelhoff, W.G. (1991), 'Information-Processing Theory and the Multinational Enterprise', *Journal of International Business Studies*, 22, No. 3, pp. 341-68.

Eitel, E.J. (1984), *Feng Shui*, (reprint) Singapore: Graham Bush

Elster, J. (1988), *Vetenskapliga förklaringar*, Göteborg: Korpen.

Engwall, L. and Vahlne, J.E. (1986), *Multinationella företag – en utmaning för ekonomisk forskning*, Stockholm: Doxa.

Far Eastern Economic Review (publisher), Hong Kong, Far Eastern Economic Review, 1984-1993, Asia Yearbook, 1983-1993.

Fligstein, N. (1985), 'The Spread of the Multidivisional Form Among Large Firms, 1919-1979', *American Sociological Review*, 50, pp. 377-91.

Forsgren, M. and Holm, U. (1991), 'Multi-Centre Structure and Location of Divisional Management in Swedish International Firms', in H. Westergaard (ed.), *An Enlarged Europe in the Global Economy*, Proceedings of the 17th Annual Conference, 15-17 December, Copenhagen, pp. 187-205.

Forsgren, M. and Pahlberg, C. (1991), 'Managing International Networks', IMP Conference Paper, Department of Business Studies, Uppsala University.

Franko, L.G. (1976), *The European Multinationals. A Renewed Challenge to American and British Big Business*, London: Harper & Row.

Ghoshal S. and Bartlett, C. (1988), 'Creation, Adoption, and Diffusion of Innovations by Subsidiaries of MNCs', *Journal of International Business Studies*, 19, No. 3, pp. 365-88.

Ghoshal, S. and Nohria, N. (1989), 'Internal Differentiation within Multinational Corporations', *Strategic Management Journal*, 10, pp. 323-37.

Ghoshal, S. and Bartlett, C. (1990), 'The Multinational Corporation as an Interorganizational Network', *Academy of Management Review*, 15, No. 4, pp. 603-25.

Glaser, B.G. (1978), *Theoretical Sensitivity*, Mill Valley, Ca: Sociology Press.

Glaser, B.G. and Strauss, A.L. (1967), *The Discovery of Grounded Theory. Strategies for Qualitative Research*, Chicago, Ill.: Aldine.

Grosse, R. (1982), 'Regional Offices in Multinational Firms', in A.T. Rugman, (ed.), *New Theories of the Multinational Enterprise*, Beckenham, Kent: Croom Helm, pp. 107-32.

Gupta, A.K. and Govindarajan, V. (1991), 'Knowledge Flows and the

Structure of Control Within Multinational Corporations', *Academy of Management Review*, 16, No. 4, pp. 768-92.

Hall, R. H. and Weiman Xu (1990), 'Research Note: Run Silent, Run Deep – Cultural Influences on Organizations in the Far East', *Organization Studies*, 11/4, pp. 569-76.

Hechter, M. (1987), *Principles of Group Solidarity*, Berkeley, Cal: University of California Press.

Hedlund, G. (1984), 'Organization In-between: The Evolution of the Mother Daughter-Structure of Managing Foreign Subsidiaries in Swedish MNCs', *Journal of International Business Studies*, XV, No. 2, pp. 109-23.

Hedlund, G. (1986), 'The Hypermodern MNC – A Heterarchy?', *Human Resource Management*, 25, No. 1, pp. 9-35.

Hedlund, G. and Åhman, P. (1984), *Managing Relationships with Foreign Subsidiaries. Organization and Control in Swedish MNCs*, Stockholm: Sveriges Mekanförbund.

Hedlund, G. and Kverneland, A. (1985), 'Are Establishment and Growth Strategies for Foreign Markets Changing?', *International Studies of Management and Organization*, XV, No. 2, pp. 41-59.

Hennart, J.F. (1982), *A Theory of Multinational Enterprise*, Ann Arbor: The University of Michigan Press.

Hodgson, G.M. (1988), *Economics and Institutions. A Manifesto for a Modern Institutional Economics*, Cambridge: Polity Press.

Hofstede, G. (1980), *Culture's Consequences: International Differences in Work-related Values*, Beverly Hills, Cal.: Sage.

Hofstede, G. (1984), 'Cultural Dimensions in Management and Planning', *Asia Pacific Journal of Management*, January, pp. 81-99.

Hofstede, G. and Bond, M. (1987), 'Confucius and Economic Growth. New Insights into Culture's Consequences', Manuscript, Institute for Research on Intercultural Cooperation.

Jansson, H. (1982), *Interfirm Linkages in a Developing Economy. The Case of Swedish Firms in India*, Acta Universitatis Upsaliensis, Studia Oeconomiae Negotiorum 14, Uppsala (dissertation).

Jansson, H. (1984),'Vertical Firm Structures and Transnational Corporations in Developing Countries', in I. Hägg and F. Wiedersheim-Paul (eds), *Between Market and Hierarchy*, Department of Business Administration, University of Uppsala, pp. 65-88.

Jansson, H. (1986), 'Purchasing Strategies of Transnational Corporations in Import Substitution Countries', in T. Cavusgil (ed.), *Advances in International Marketing*, Volume 1, Greenwich, Conn.: JAI Press.

Jansson, H. (1987), *Affärskulturer och relationer. En studie av svenska industriföretag i Sydöstasien*, MTC skriftserie nr. 29, Stockholm: Liber.

Jansson, H. (1988), *Strategier och organisation på avlägsna marknader*, Lund: Studentlitteratur.

Jansson, H. (1989), 'Internationalization Processes in South-East Asia: An Extension or Another Process?', in E. Kaynak and K-H. Lee (eds), *Global Business. Asia Pacific Dimensions*, London: Routledge, pp. 78-102.

Jansson, H. (1991), 'Organization of Transactions in Distant Markets: The Case of Swedish TNCs in South East Asia', in C-H. Wee and T-K. Hui (eds), *Proceedings of the Academy of International Business Southeast Asia Conference*, 20-22 June, National University of Singapore, pp. 47-55.

Jansson, H. (1993), *Industrial Products: A Guide to the International Marketing Economics Model*, New York/London/Norwood: The Haworth Press.

Jansson, H. and Sharma, D.S. (1993), 'Industrial Policy Liberalization and TNCs: The Indian Experience', *Scandinavian Journal of Management*, 9, No. 2, pp. 129-143.

Jansson, H., Sharma, D.S. and Saqib, M. (1993), 'Network Strategies toward Governments. Transnational Corporations and the Indian Government', Manuscript, Lund: Institute of Economic Research, School of Economics and Business Administration.

Johanson, J. and Wiedersheim-Paul, F. (1975), 'The Internationalization of the Firm – Four Swedish Cases', *Journal of Management Studies*, 12, October, pp. 305-22.

Johanson, J. and Mattsson, L.G. (1987), 'Internationalization in Industrial Systems – A Network Approach', in N. Hood and J.E. Vahlne (eds), *Strategies in Global Competition*, Chichester: Wiley.

Khin, M.K. (1988), 'APJM and Comparative Management in Asia', *Asia Pacific Journal of Management*, 5, No. 3, pp. 207-224.

Kindleberger, C.P. (1969), *American Business Abroad*, New Haven, Conn.: Yale University Press.

Kirchbach, F. von (1983), *Economic Policies Towards Transnational Corporations*, Baden-Baden: Nomos Verlagsgesellschaft.

Kogut, B. (1985), 'A Critique of Transaction Cost Economics as a Theory of Organizational Behaviour', Working Paper 85-05, The Wharton School, University of Pennsylvania, Philadelphia, Pa.

Lall, S. (1983), *The New Multinationals*, New York: Wiley.

Larsson, A. (1985), *Structure and Change. Power in the Trans-*

national Enterprise, Acta Universitatis Upsaliensis, Studia Oeconomiae Negotiorum 23, Uppsala (dissertation).

Larsson, B. (1989), *Koncernföretaget*, Stockholm: EFI, Stockholm School of Economics.

Lasserre, P. (1988), 'Corporate Strategic Management and the Overseas Chinese Groups', *Asia Pacific Journal of Management*, 5, No. 2, January, pp. 115-31.

Leblebici, H. (1985), 'Transactions and Organizational Forms: A Reanalysis', *Journal of Organization Studies*, 6, No. 2, pp. 97-115.

Lim, L.Y.C. and Gosling, P. (eds) (1983), *The Chinese in Southeast Asia*, Singapore: Maruzen Asia.

Limligan, V.S. (1986), *The Overseas Chinese in ASEAN: Business Strategies and Management Practices*, Manila: VITA Development Company.

Lip, E. (1989), *Feng Shui for Business*, Singapore: Times.

Lundgren, S. and Hedlund, G. (1983), *Svenska företag i Sydöstasien*, Stockholm: Institute of International Business Research, Stockholm School of Economics.

McManus, J. (1975), 'The Cost of Alternative Economic Organizations', *Canadian Journal of Economics*, 75, pp. 334-50.

Magee, S.P. (1977), 'Information and the Multinational Corporation: An Appropriability Theory of Foreign Direct Investment', in J.N. Bhagwati (ed.), *The New International Economic Order*, Cambridge, Mass: MIT Press, pp. 123-35.

Mahini, A. and Wells, L.T. (1986), 'Government Relations in the Global Firm', in M. Porter (ed.), *Competition in Global Industries*, Boston, Mass: Harvard Business School Press, pp. 291-312.

Martinez, J.I. and Jarillo, J.C. (1989), 'The Evolution of Research on Coordination Mechanisms in Multinational Corporations', *Journal of International Business Studies*, 20, No. 3, pp. 489-514.

Martinez, J.I. and Jarillo, J.C. (1991), 'Coordination Demands of International Strategies', *Journal of International Business Studies*, 22, No. 3, pp. 429-44.

Meyer, J.W. and Scott, W.R. (1983), *Organizational Environments. Ritual and Rationality*, Beverly Hills, Cal: Sage.

Milton-Smith, J. (1985), 'Japanese Management Overseas: International Business Strategy and the Case of Singapore', paper, The Enterprise and Management in East Asia Conference, Hong Kong.

Mintzberg, H. (1987), 'Crafting Strategy', *Harvard Business Review*, No. 4, pp. 66-75.

Mintzberg, H. and Waters, J.A., (1985), 'Of Strategies, Deliberate and Emergent', *Strategic Management Journal*, Vol. 6, pp. 257-72.

Monteverde, K. and Teece, D.J. (1982), 'Supplier Switching Costs and Vertical Integration in the Automobile Industry', *Bell Journal of Economics*, pp. 206-13.

Myrdal, G. 1968, *Asian Drama – An Inquiry into the Poverty of Nations*, Vol. I-III, New York: Twentieth Century Fund.

Nicholas, S. (1983), 'Agency Contracts, Institutional Modes, and the Transition to Foreign Direct Investment by British Manufacturing Multinationals Before 1939', *Journal of Economic History*, XLIII, No. 3.

Nicholas, S. (1986), 'The Theory of Multinational Enterprise as a Transactional Mode', in P. Hertner and G. Jones (eds) *Multinationals - Theory and History*, Aldershot: Gower Press.

North, D. (1978), 'Structure and Performance: The Task of Economic History', *Journal of Economic Literature*, 16, pp. 129-41.

Ouchi, W.G. (1980), 'Markets, Bureaucracies and Clans', *Administrative Science Quarterly*, 25, pp. 129-41.

Palmer, D., Friedland, R., Jennings, P.D. and Powers, M.E. (1987), 'The Economics and Politics of Structure: The Multidivisional Form and the Large U.S. Corporation', *Administrative Science Quarterly*, 32, pp. 25-48.

Parry, T.G. (1985), 'Internalisation as a General Theory of Foreign Direct Investment: A Critique', *Weltwirtschaftliches Archiv*, 121, pp. 564-9.

Perrow, C. (1986), *Complex Organizations: A Critical Essay*, 3rd edition, New York: Random House.

Pfeffer, J. (1981), *Power in Organizations*, Marshfield, Mass.: Pitman.

Pfeffer, J. and Salancik, G.R. (1978), *The External Control of Organizations – A Resource Dependence Perspective*, New York: Harper and Row.

Porter, M. (1980), *Competitive Strategy. Techniques for Analyzing Industries and Competitors*, New York: The Free Press.

Porter, M. (1981), 'The Contributions of Industrial Organization to Strategic Management', *Academy of Management Review*, 6, pp. 609-20.

Porter, M. (1986), 'Competition in Global Industries: A Conceptual Framework', in M. Porter (ed.), *Competition in Global Industries*, Boston, Mass.: Harvard Business School Press, pp. 15-60.

Prahalad, C.K. and Doz, Y.L. (1987), *The Multinational Mission.*

Balancing Local Demands and Global Vision, New York: The Free Press.

Pye, L.W. (1985), *Asian Power and Politics. The Cultural Dimensions of Authority*, Cambridge: Belknap Press.

Redding, S.G. (1980), 'Cognition as an Aspect of Culture and its Relation to Management Processes: An Exploratory View of the Chinese Case', *Journal of Management Studies*, 17, No. 2, pp. 127-48.

Redding, S.G. and Ng, M. (1983), 'The Role of Face in the Organizational Perceptions of Chinese Managers', *International Studies of Management and Organization*, No. 3, pp. 92-123.

Redding, S.G. and Pugh, D. (1985), 'The Formal and the Informal: Japanese and Chinese Organization Structures', paper, The Enterprise and Management in East Asia Conference, Hong Kong.

Redding, S.G. and Wong, G.Y.Y. (1986), 'Chinese Organizational Behaviour', in M.H.B. Bond (ed.), *The Psychology of the Chinese People*, Hong Kong: Oxford University Press, pp. 267-95.

Robins, J.A. (1987), 'Organizational Economics: Notes on the Use of Transaction-Cost Theory in the Study of Organizations', *Administrative Science Quarterly*, 32, pp. 68-86.

Robock, S.H. and Simmonds, K. (1989), *International Business and Multinational Enterprises*, Homewood, Ill.: Irwin.

Rugman, A.T. (1980) 'Internalization as a General Theory of Foreign Direct Investment: A Reappraisal of the Literature', *Weltwirtschaftliches Archiv*, 116, pp. 365-79.

Rugman, A.T. (1981), *Inside the Multinationals: The Economics of Internal Markets*, New York: Columbia University Press.

Rugman, A.T. (ed.) (1982), *New Theories of the Multinational Enterprise*, Beckenham, Kent: Croom Helm.

Scott, W.R. (1987), 'The Adolescence of Institutional Theory', *Administrative Science Quarterly*, 32, pp. 493-511.

Senkuttuvan, A. (ed.) (1981), *MNCs and ASEAN Development in the 1980s*, Singapore: Institute of Southeast Studies.

Simon, H. (1989), *Price Management*, Amsterdam: Elsevier Science Publishers.

Sjöstrand, S.-E. (1985), *Samhällsorganisation. En ansats till en institutionell ekonomisk mikroteori*, Lund: Doxa.

Sjöstrand, S.-E. (1992), 'On the Rationale behind "Irrational" Institutions, *Journal of Economic Issues*, XXVI, No. 4, pp. 1007-40.

Smith, C., Whipp, R. and Willmott, H. (1988), 'Case-Study Research in Accounting: Methodological Breakthrough or Ideological Weapon?', *Advances in Public Interest Accounting*, 2, pp. 95-120.

Stening, B.W. and Everett, J.E. (1984), 'Japanese Managers in Southeast Asia: Amiable Superstars or Arrogant Upstarts?', *Asia Pacific Journal of Management*, 1, No. 3, pp. 171-80.

Stopford, J.M. and Wells Jr, L.T. (1972), *Managing the Multinational Enterprise*, New York: Basic Books.

Teece, D.J. (1981), 'The Multinational Enterprise: Market Failure and Market Power Considerations', *Sloan Management Review*, 22, pp. 3-17.

Teece, D.J. (1983), 'Multinational Enterprise, Internal Governance, and Industrial Organization', *The American Economic Review*, 75, pp. 233-7.

Teece, D.J. (1986), 'Transaction Cost Economics and the Multinational Enterprise. An Assessment', *Journal of Economic Behaviour and Organization*, 7, pp. 21-45.

Thompson, S. and M. Wright (eds) (1988), *Internal Organization, Efficiency and Profit*, Oxford: Philip Allan Publishers.

Villacorta, W.V. (1976), 'The Chinese in Southeast Asia: An Introduction', *Philippine Sociological Review*, 24, No. 1-4, pp. 5-16.

Walker, G. and Weber, D. (1984), 'A Transaction Cost Approach to Make-or-Buy Decisions', *Administrative Science Quarterly*, 29, pp. 373-91.

Whitley, R. (1990), 'Eastern Asian Enterprise Structures and the Comparative Analysis of Forms of Business Organization', *Organization Studies*, 11, No. 1, pp. 47-74.

Whitley, R. (1992), *Business Systems in East Asia*, London: Sage.

Williamson, O.E. (1975), *Markets and Hierarchies: Analysis and Antitrust Implications*, New York: The Free Press.

Williamson, O.E. (1979), 'Transaction-Cost Economics: the Governance of Contractual Relations', *Journal of Law and Economics*, 22, October, pp. 3-61.

Williamson, O.E. (1981), 'The Modern Corporation: Origins, Evolution, Attributes', *Journal of Economic Literature*, 19, December, pp. 1537-68.

Williamson, O.E. (1985), *The Economic Institutions of Capitalism. Firms, Markets, Relational Contracting*, New York: The Free Press.

Williamson, O.E. (1986), 'Economics and Sociology: Promoting a Dialog', Working Paper 49, Yale Law School.

Williamson, O.E. (1989), 'Internal Economic Organization', in A. Malm (ed.), *Perspectives on the Economics of Organization*, Lund: Institute of Economic Research.

Williamson, O.E. and Ouchi, W.G. (1981), 'The Markets and Hierarchies and Visible Hand Perspectives', in A.H. Van de Ven and W.F. Joyce (eds), *Perspectives on Organization Design and Behaviour*, New York: Wiley, pp. 347-70.

Wimalasiri, J. (1988), 'Cultural Influence on Aspects of Management: The Experience of the Chinese in Singapore', *Asia Pacific Journal of Management*, 5, No. 3, pp. 180-96.

Winship, C. and Rosen, S. (1988), 'Introduction: Sociological and Economic Approaches to the Analysis of Social Structure', *American Journal of Sociology*, 94, Supplement, pp. 1-16.

Yin, R.Y. (1984/89), *Case Study Research: Design and Methods*, Beverly Hills, Cal.: Sage.

Index